Americana
in 1/12 Scale

50 AUTHENTIC PROJECTS

Americana
in 1/12 Scale

50 AUTHENTIC PROJECTS

MARY LOU SANTOVEC
& JOANN OGREENC

GUILD OF MASTER CRAFTSMAN PUBLICATIONS

First published 2002 by

Guild of Master Craftsman Publications Ltd,

166 High Street, Lewes,

East Sussex, BN7 1XN

ISBN 1 86108 248 7

Cover and finished item photography by Anthony Bailey, GMC Publications Photographic Studio
(to whom many thanks are due for his tireless and creative photographic efforts)
Photograph of Mary Lou Santovec courtesy of Kevin Harnack
Design by John Round at Lovelock & Co, Brighton
Cover design by Olly Prentice, GMC Publications Design Studio
Illustrations by John Yates from original drawings by JoAnn Ogreenc

Typeface: Humana Sans and Foundry

Colour origination by Viscan Graphics (Singapore)

Printed and bound by
Sun Fung Offset Binding Co Ltd, China

To Jim, for his loving support and interest in all my projects. And to my mom, Virginia, for helping me to develop an interest in miniatures.

JoAnn

To Rick, for his unconditional love and support during this very 'tiny' project. To JoAnn, who introduced me to the magical world of miniatures and without whom this book would not be a reality. To my musician extraordinaire who rekindles my spirit. And to my muse, my inspiration, my angel – by believing in me, you gave me my voice.

Mary Lou

Contents

Introduction

Readers of *Gulliver's Travels* marvel at Jonathan Swift's account of his hero's adventures in the land of Lilliput, where the inhabitants and the surroundings are only six inches high. While Lilliput exists only in the reader's imagination, there is a place where everything is smaller than real life – the world of miniatures.

A miniature is a small version of a full-size object, and miniaturists generally work in one of three common sizes, or scales: 1/12, 1/24 and 1/48. To give you a better idea of how these work, if a miniature object is made in 1/12 scale, it means that one inch represents one foot of the full-size object; if working in 1/24 scale, half an inch in miniature translates to one foot full-size, and for 1/48 scale, a quarter inch equals one foot full-size (and will probably require a magnifying glass and ample bright light to assemble some of the parts).

Almost anything that exists in real life can be reproduced in miniature. Miniaturists pride themselves on making an object look as authentic as possible and, for those who strive for this level of realism, the ultimate goal is to make the finished piece look identical to the real thing – just smaller.

As more and more people discover the magic of miniatures, the quality of craftsmanship continues to rise. Miniatures are no longer perceived as children's playthings and have evolved to the level of an art form. Every year, organizations such as the International Guild of Miniature Artisans (IGMA) review the work of new miniaturists and invite those whose work is of the highest calibre of craftsmanship to join.

Many miniaturists first discover the hobby as a child when, one Christmas morning, they waken to find a doll's house under the tree. While some of these doll's house owners move on to different hobbies, for others it is the beginning of a lifelong passion for small worlds. So, whether you have indulged in the love affair from childhood, or have discovered it as an adult, miniatures is a hobby that knows no age limit.

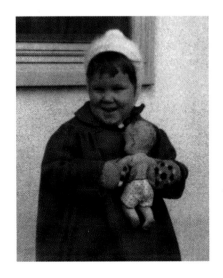

Mary Lou's passion for all things tiny began at an early age

In addition to generating excitement for established miniaturists, we hope this book will be a starting point for a new set of miniaturists: we've tried to make the projects as accessible as possible for those with relatively few craft skills.

This is a step-by-step book, therefore much work went into the development of the designs, each of which was created specifically for this book. JoAnn designed and crafted the items, as well as drafting the instructions and illustrations. We provide you with a list of the equipment and materials you need to complete the project. And, with a few exceptions, we've included entries for recommended glues, paints and polymer clays. Alongside the technical information, there is historical and cultural information on the origin of the project's full-sized counterpart and, where applicable, how it is used today. Finally, we also offer suggestions as to how you might incorporate a particular item into a scene or dolls' house. Our goal is to make the book entertaining, informative and accessible for both miniaturists and non-hobbyists alike.

We encourage you to follow our instructions and adapt them to your individual needs. Perhaps you'd like to paint your Southwestern sun face with vibrant yellows and reds instead of terracotta. Feel free to combine and change to create your own piece of Americana. For those inspired readers who want to build on their knowledge of the hobby, we have provided a list of resources and a comprehensive bibliography at the back of the book.

Every one of the projects is conceived in 1/12 scale. They are accessible to both the beginner and the intermediate hobbyist. For the beginner to miniature-making, we've ordered the projects in each 'Americana' chapter in order of complexity, the most straightforward first. In some cases, however, we have wandered from this in favor of logic: for example, the baseball pennant and hat are grouped together, even though the the latter is complex enough to appear later in the chapter. This affords you some freedom to work forward or backward as you wish.

The supplies are widely available from craft and dolls' house retailers and mail order suppliers. Where possible, JoAnn (an avid recycler), adapted an item from something else: an old leather driving glove earned a new life as a pair of miniature moccasins, and the remnants of an old flannel shirt became a cowboy's bedroll. We encourage you to take the same approach to your own miniature work. While many items are relatively inexpensive to buy, you will find that saving on materials where you can will be of great benefit.

You are invited to try one or all of the projects. Once smitten by the miniatures bug, we guarantee you will never look at a full-sized object again without thinking: "I could make that in miniature".

We hope that you enjoy creating these projects as much as we did developing them, and bringing them to you in this book. Welcome to the wonderful, magical world of miniatures.

Mary Lou Santovec

JoAnn Ogreenc

What is Americana?

The American ideal has always been to welcome peoples of diverse cultural origins; to allow them the political, religious and economic freedoms they left their own homelands to find in the 'Land of the free'.

As they journeyed into an unknown future, early newcomers brought with them the richness of their unique cultures: their traditions and cherished objects. These things were used daily in their homes and characterized their neighborhoods and have, over time, come to be known as 'American'.

Many early rituals and objects were appropriated directly from the Native Americans who helped the first European settlers adjust to their new environment. Others were developed over time, according to utility, as the newcomers migrated west across the country and evolved new communities and ways of living.

For many, the traditional understanding of 'Americana' is commonly understood to mean 'colonial'. The homes of the first

The pilgrims are greeted by Massosoit, chief of the Pokanokets, 1620

13 founding colonies of immigrants offer a wealth of inspiration for new and/or adapted household goods and accessories. But this is only one notion of 'Americana'. Our definition is slightly different. America is truly a melting pot of cultures, and we have deliberately focused a wider lens on the country's diversity, thus giving 'Americana' a broader interpretation. Instead of featuring only colonial items, we've included chapters on everyday objects from five different aspects of American history and culture: the Native Americans, rural America, the old West, nostalgic America and sporting America.

As a result, we hope that the reader discovers an inspiring, diverse collection of miniatures to tempt them. Where else would you find both a beanbag chair and a rural rug beater, a Pueblo storyteller and a bowling ball and bag in the same volume?

We've also included artifacts from a variety of eras: some date back to pre-colonial times, others are more contemporary. Whether you favor the traditional or the funky, the sublime or the outrageous, we intend to offer something to appeal to all tastes.

We began this project with a list of 99 items, from which we selected 50. The difficulty of this exercise, we realized, is defining what makes up the 'American experience', and concluded that it is a bricolage of the traditional and the eclectic. Projects like the aluminum Christmas tree represent an aspect of childhood tradition rooted in the 1950s which endured into the 1960s and 1970s. The popcorn and cranberry chains form part of a longer American tradition which continues today.

While researching the projects, we were fascinated to find that many of them have actually been around, in one form or another, for thousands of years. For example, did you know that the Egyptians were the first to throw a round stone at a group of similar objects: the precursor to what is known today as bowling? Or that the Romans developed an early version of the United States Postal Service?

'Americana' encompasses a diverse historical and cultural mix and this offers many exciting possibilities for making miniature versions of artifacts in the 'real' world.

Getting started

One of the first considerations for the new miniaturist is his or her work space: it needs to be practical, comfortable, clean and well-ventilated. It is also imperative to have a good light source. When you're working with items that are $\frac{1}{64}$in thick, it is essential that you are able to see them clearly. A magnifying source can be very helpful.

Keeping an orderly work space

Organization is key. When you work with miniature objects, there is always a risk of losing or damaging the materials and projects. Even worse: with small pieces, you might cause injury and harm to yourself, your loved ones or pets.

But how can you keep chaos and clutter from taking over? It is ideal to have a dedicated work space for your miniature work, but this is not always feasible. To keep your tools and materials handy, we suggest building up a range of different-sized containers to store and organize materials and half-finished projects. Reuse or recycle storage containers where possible rather than continually purchasing new ones.

Organization tips

- Use clear plastic 35mm film canisters to store jewelry findings, beads, small shells and other tiny items. The tight-fitting caps will keep the objects from spilling should you accidentally knock one over. And the plastic canister will not break if you drop it.
- Check your pharmacy for one-a-day plastic pill containers, which are available in two different capacities: a week's or a month's supply. Many of them have flip-top lids that make stored items easily accessible. The snap-down action of these lids also helps to prevent spillage if accidentally knocked over.
- Acquire a second-hand spice rack and bottles. Some racks can be

wall-mounted, others revolve on a turntable. The rack means items are accessible, and the glass bottles let you see what is inside.

◆ Store sand and stones in metal coffee containers with plastic lids: the metal holds up better to the roughness of the materials.

◆ Invest in a series of different-sized, transparent plastic containers with well-fitting covers. Some are large enough to contain a pair of shoes, others to hold sweaters. These are great for storing half-finished projects and larger items, such as basswood, wallpaper and tools. Plastic fishing tackle containers have sections that keep items tidy. Tight-fitting covers protect against dust and humidity.

◆ Turn plastic hardware storage containers that hold nuts and bolts into handy mini filing cabinets. The containers come with plastic pull-out drawers and can be labeled for quick retrieval of items.

◆ An old emery board or nailfile glued to the work space makes a handy pencil sharpener.

◆ Storing glue bottles upside down makes them easy to pour when needed. To make a convenient storage rack, drill bottleneck-sized holes into a piece of wood and then invert the bottles so that the nozzles fit through the pre-drilled holes.

◆ Keep a wet rag handy to clean up paint and glue spills. Store it in a container with a snap-on lid.

Workshop safety tips

◆ Keep a first-aid kit and a fire extinguisher close at hand in case of an accident.

◆ Keep chemical substances and sharp objects such as needles and craft knives away from children or pets.

◆ Read the label and the instructions on the container. Besides listing directions for use, product labels also contain information about health hazards, appropriate equipment and safety tips. Reading the warning labels can prevent unnecessary accidents and save time.

◆ Always use paints, solvents and glues in a well-ventilated area.

◆ When working with solvents, wear gloves. Many of these products can be absorbed through the skin.

◆ Do not mix different chemical products together unless the instructions on the packaging specifically state that it is safe to do so.

NOTE
When working with paints, solvents and glues, safety is paramount. Remember: these are potentially harmful chemicals and should be treated with respect.

When sanding, use dust masks to protect you from potentially harmful effects

Certain non-toxic products can become toxic when used in combination.

◆ Keep paints, solvents and glues away from heat sources and exposed flames.

◆ Discard solvent- or paint-soaked rags in an appropriate – preferably metal – container. A rag that has been used to apply stain can spontaneously combust if left exposed to the air.

◆ The old adage: 'measure twice, cut once' will limit the possibility of unhappy results.

◆ When storing products, store them in their original containers. If that is not feasible, make sure that the container to which you transfer the product is clean, does not react to the contents and is clearly labeled.

◆ When sanding, wear a dust mask or respirator to protect your lungs from harmful particles.

◆ Finally, many incidents can be prevented by ensuring your work space remains clean and tidy.

Tools and materials

Whether you are just beginning your adventure into miniatures or have been at it for some time, creating your own miniature objects is easier if you have the right tools. The majority of the projects in this book can be made using a few basic tools and materials, most of which are readily available from hardware or craft stores.

Basic miniatures tool kit

Your kit should ideally contain the following:

◆ A pair of needle-nose pliers

◆ A metal straight-edged ruler. Do not use a plastic or wooden ruler; the metal variety allows you to scribe perfectly straight lines and check the flatness of surfaces

◆ A wire cutter

◆ Several pairs of scissors. Reserve one specifically for cutting paper, which dulls scissor blades, and one for cutting fabric

◆ Sandpaper in various grades

◆ A pin vise with small drill bits

◆ Paintbrushes of various sizes

◆ A tack cloth to brush off dust particles from sanded items

- Clamps in various sizes. Tiny clothes pins or clamps used to close snack and freezer bags work well for holding small parts together while waiting for glue to dry
- Toothpicks, bamboo skewers and wooden craft sticks for applying paint and glue
- Single-edged razor blades for slicing polymer clay
- Cotton swabs, or buds, for applying paint
- A craft knife with a No. 11 blade and replacement blades in various sizes
- Sewing needles
- Dressmaker's and corsage pins
- Rags, baby wipes or paper towels for quick clean-ups
- Latex gloves. We prefer the thin, disposable kind that allow you to pick up tiny pieces without having to remove your gloves
- Rubber bands
- Tweezers
- Cellophane and masking tape
- PVA and cyanoacrylate glues
- An awl to make holes in wood, leather or plastic
- A piece of ceramic tile for baking polymer clay. If not, substitute with sheets of aluminum foil
- Sharp pencils and a pencil sharpener
- An eraser
- A fine-tipped black permanent marker
- Circular templates of various sizes, ranging between $1/16$ (0.1cm) and 1in (2.5cm). These are available from craft stores or obtained from engineering and architectural suppliers.

Optional extras

As you progress with your miniatures, you may wish to acquire other dedicated tools such as miniature table saws, lathes and drills.

Polymer clay

Polymer clay is the workhorse of the miniatures world. Unlike an earth-based clay such as ceramic clay, polymer clay is a modeling compound comprised of tiny grains of polyvinyl chloride (PVC), coloring agents, resins and plasticizers. The Eberhard-Faber Company, best known for its writing accessories and art supplies,

A versatile medium, polymer clay is available in a wide range of brands and colors

created the product in 1930 and today, it has an unrivaled status among craftspeople for whom it is *the* material for making miniatures.

The medium is versatile. It can be made to resemble a variety of materials, including porcelain, wood, stone and glass. It is easily manipulable and comes in an assortment of colors.

Polymer clay is sold under various brand names, including: Cernit, Sculpey, Super Sculpey, Premo Sculpey, Sculpey III, Granitex, Fimo and Friendly Clay. (Promat polymer clay is no longer available.) They all have slightly differing properties and hardening temperatures, but can be mixed together to achieve a specific effect. As a guide, we have specified brands we have used ourselves for a project, but others may be substituted as appropriate.

Polymer clays are soft and pliable at room temperature. Most brands require a little conditioning to become workable. To condition the clay, simply knead it until it becomes soft and easy to use. Some miniaturists prefer to run the clay through a pasta machine or, for firmer clays, to use a liquid softening agent. Once softened, the clay can be sculpted with modeling tools, be rolled or cut with a sharp, single-edged razor blade. Unused clay should be stored in a cool place, preferably a refrigerator or freezer.

Unlike ceramic clays, polymer clays do not dry out with exposure to air. To harden, they must be baked in a conventional or toaster oven. Polymer clays do not cure well in a microwave oven. Using this type of hardening process gives miniaturists a great deal of creative freedom; they can repeatedly change direction before deciding on the look of the finished product.

Once baked, polymer clay can be painted, drilled, sanded, glazed, glued or otherwise decorated to the desired effect.

Polymer clay safety tips

- Follow the manufacturer's directions on the packaging.
- When baking, place the clay object on a ceramic tile. Pyrex dishes, baking trays or pieces of aluminum foil also work well.
- Avoid overbaking the clay.
- Always ensure there is good ventilation in the kitchen or workroom and do not inhale the fumes emitted during baking.
- If you use a piece of cookware for baking, such as a cookie sheet, do not use it for baking food, too.

Glues and adhesives

With all the work that a miniaturist puts into a project, the last thing you want to happen is to have the object fall apart because you used the wrong type of glue.

Glues and adhesives were originally made from animal hides and fish parts. But modern chemistry has given us a plethora of products, as a trip to the craft store will reveal. With all the options, how do you choose the most appropriate glue or adhesive for your project?

The first thing to remember is that no single brand of glue works well for all materials. The key to a good bond is to select a product that works with the types of materials you need to adhere.

PVA glues

A multipurpose polyvinyl acetate (PVA) white glue can be used for materials with porous or semi-porous surfaces such as wood, fabric, leather or paper. PVA glue is nontoxic, odorless, nonflammable and sets quickly. It also dries clear and cleans up with water.

Because they do not bond instantly like other glues, PVA glues have a chance to permeate a porous surface and produce a stronger bond than fast-setting glues. PVA glues also give you more time to align the parts before the glue hardens, which can be important when working with tiny pieces.

Tacky glue is a variation of a PVA glue. These glues are specially formulated for a quick bond. They offer a variety of drying times and can be substituted for a multipurpose PVA glue in most situations.

Aliphatic or wood glues

Aliphatic resins or yellow wood glues produce a stronger bond and have a faster setting time than their PVA cousins. Aliphatic glues are nontoxic, odorless and clean up with water. They do not dry as clear as PVA glues, but yellow wood glues can be sanded once dry.

Hot-melt glues

Hot-melt glues come in waxy sticks and are applied with an electric glue gun. Objects glued with hot-melt glues bond almost instantly. Hot-melt glues can be used on wood, metal, ceramics and cloth. For a more permanent bond, manufacturers recommend that you do not apply hot-melt glue to a cold surface. To ensure the bond is effective, first warm the surface with an electric hair dryer or other controllable heat source before applying the glue. Again, have some regard for safety and read the manufacturer's label before you begin.

Cyanoacrylate glues

Instant bond glues are made from cyanogen and acrylic resins and are often grouped together in the category of cyanoacrylate glues. These glues bond surfaces together within a few seconds. Their quick setting time usually means clamping is unnecessary.

These glues come in two forms: liquid and gel, and are often called superglues. Liquid superglues work well on hard, nonporous surfaces such as glass, metal, plastic or ceramic, whereas gel superglues work best for porous and semi-porous surfaces. The downside is that these glues do not allow for repositioning or refitting of parts. If they get on your hands, it is extremely difficult to remove them without damaging your skin. Superglues do not bond well with foam rubber, Teflon, polyethylene and polypropylene.

To get the quick adhesion of a superglue with the stronger bond of a PVA glue, combine the two simultaneously on the surfaces you want to bond together.

Solvent glues

Solvent glues, such as E-6000, are often a good choice for gluing polymer clay. These glues are quick-bonding, reasonably fast-drying (most set in 24 hours) and dry clear and flexible. Because they're solvent-based, these glues cannot be cleaned up with water.

Fusibles

Fusible products are adhesives rather than glues. Fusibles such as Pellon's Wonder-Under apply an adhesive to a surface when the fusible is melted with a heat source, for example: an iron. They are a useful alternative to sewing and can be used to bond fabric to paper, cardboard or wood.

Sealants

Thread and fiber sealants, such as Fray Check by Dritz, are types of glue that seal loose threads or the edges of fabric to prevent them from unraveling.

Gluing tips

◆ Read the label. Get to know the product and any safety-related issues. Always follow the manufacturer's instructions.

◆ Whenever possible, choose a latex-based rather than a solvent-based glue. Latex-based glues are generally nontoxic, do not emit fumes and are easy to clean up. Solvent-based glues are highly flammable, toxic if ingested, and can be absorbed through the skin. They also require a solvent to clean up.

◆ Make sure the surfaces you want to glue are clean, dry and free from debris or oil. The oil from your fingertips is often enough to discourage a good bond. Wipe down surfaces before applying a dab of glue to help ensure a successful result.

◆ Test the surfaces you want to bond before applying the glue. We encourage you to dry-fit the pieces (assemble them without any glue to see if they fit together properly) and then test the glue on a scrap of the same material to ensure that you are using the appropriate product for the job.

◆ Store any opened glue properly. It is not worth trying to save a few pennies by using old glue. Reseal any open glue. A thin coating of petroleum jelly on the threads of the tube will keep the cap from sticking. After each use, clean any excess glue from the inside of the cap.

Paint

The project is assembled, the glue is dry and now comes the fun part – adding a coat of paint to your miniature object. Much like glues and adhesives, craft paints come in a range of types and brands.

Acrylic

The most commonly used type of paint for miniatures work is acrylic paint. This all-purpose, water-based paint is nontoxic, permanent, fast-drying, adheres to a variety of materials, comes in a rainbow of colours and is easy to clean up.

Opaque colours generally cover in one coat. If you want a more translucent effect, thin the acrylic paint with a little water. One brand of acrylic paint can also be mixed with others to achieve a specific shade. As with any product, it is important to read the label before use. If in doubt as to whether acrylic paint is the best choice to

A selection of enamel paints and brushes

achieve a specific effect for a particular project, first test some on a scrap piece of material that you do not wish to use afterwards.

Enamel

For slick and slippery surfaces, for example: glass, tile, ceramics and primed metal, enamel paint adheres better than acrylic paint. Choose a durable air-dry paint; in other words, one that does not require heat-setting. Test it on a scrap piece first to check that it produces the desired effect.

Varnish

To add a shine to your finished object, brush on a coat of acrylic-based artist's varnish using a clean, dry synthetic-bristled flat brush. An acrylic-based varnish forms a tough, flexible film that adds protection to a painted surface. It also provides a clear, non-yellowing finish. Acrylic-based artist's varnishes have no fumes, are easy to clean up and are not tacky when dry. Acrylic varnishes are ideal for indoor items. Polyurethane varnishes provide extra protection outdoors for objects exposed to the elements.

Americana
Projects

Native American

Birch bark basket ★ Reed basket

Trade beads ★ Dream catcher

Wrapped feather ★ God's eye

Cornhusk doll ★ Moccasins

Southwest sun faces ★ Pueblo storyteller

While history books argue about which explorer first discovered America - Leif Erickson, Christopher Columbus or some unknown early ancient mariner - the inhabitants that greeted the first white man were the ancestors of today's Native Americans.

Historians believe that at some point during the Ice Age the ancient tribes lived in and around Siberia. Some 15,000 years ago, these tribes eventually moved east across a bridge of land from Siberia to Alaska.

The tribes' decision to move on was a matter of life and death. They were forced to follow migrating herds of animals in order to survive. Often, travelers decided to

Life in a Comanche village, circa 1830. Animal skins were used to perform many functions – the most important being to provide shelter

make their home somewhere *en route* across the continent. Others continued south and east. The descendents of these brave explorers would eventually make their way across North America.

As they settled in new places, these ancient peoples had to adapt their ways of living to different climates and terrain. Hunting eventually gave way to land cultivation and fishing. Homes were constructed from found materials: mud and twigs, animal skins, caves and rock shelters.

In each place, tribes formed new communities, each with distinct cultures and traditions. Christopher Columbus called the descendents of these ancient peoples Indians, believing, quite mistakenly, that he had discovered the East Indies. In fact, he had landed on the North American continent at San Salvador in the Virgin Islands. Today, these peoples are more properly honored as Native Americans.

Secotan village, North Carolina, circa 1585. Native Americans cultivated their land to produce food for the whole community

Baskets

No single culture can claim to have developed the basket. Many forms of woven containers have been around for thousands of years, and predate ceramic vessels. Baskets have been found in the tombs of the early Egyptians, and there are many references to them in the Bible, including the notable example used to carry Moses down the Nile.

Native Americans used baskets for gathering, preparing, storing and even cooking food. Tribes in the Southwest wove baskets to use as water bottles, ingeniously waterproofing them with a coating of tree pitch. Some baskets were even designed solely for ceremonial use.

Making baskets required highly developed skills, and harvesting and preparing the right materials was key. Baskets have been made from plant fibers of all kinds, for example: yucca, cattails, cornhusks, splints from trees, and pine needles. Once gathered and prepared, basketmakers would plait, coil or twine the fibers into functional containers.

Baskets had two advantages over pottery: they were unbreakable and lightweight – a key benefit for nomadic tribes. And because they were made out of plant fibers, they could be adapted from available natural resources.

Birch bark basket

One of the native plants that yielded good materials for basket-making was the paper or white birch tree. White birch bark was readily available, waterproof, pliable and resistant to rot.

Removing the bark from a living birch tree could potentially kill it. Thus, the Native Americans took care to work around this by gathering the bark from fallen trees in late spring and early summer while the bark was at its thickest, and the top layer literally peeled away from the tree.

To store the birch bark, the Native Americans would lay the bark flat on the ground and place weights on the pieces to prevent them from curling.

The basket would be sewn with white spruce roots or the inner bark of a cedar tree. Rims would be added to birch bark baskets for decoration as well as for reinforcing fragile parts of the bark.

Some tribes would use birch bark baskets for cooking. Hot stones were placed in the basket along with the food. They were also good for berry picking; the chemicals found in the bark prevented the berries from growing mold.

For authenticity, store mini berries or stew in your birch bark basket and place it in a Native American scene.

Tools and materials

Photocopy paper (white)
Acrylic paint (white, black and raw sienna)
A facial tissue (white)
Cotton thread (dark brown)
Cotton floss (candlewicking thread) (light brown)
Compass or 1½in (3.8cm) circular template
Scissors
Fine sewing needle
Paintbrush
Pencil
PVA glue
Small bowl with water

Finished size

1in (2.5cm) high and ⅜in (1cm) in diameter

METHOD

1 Make a dilution of the raw sienna acrylic paint and a small amount of water to an approximate ratio of 1:3. Lightly paint an area about 4in (10cm) square on one side of the photocopy paper.

2 To resemble lines on the bark, add a few light strokes of black paint before the raw sienna paint dries, and blend with a clean paintbrush. Allow to dry.

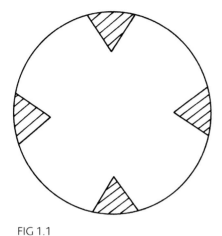

FIG 1.1

3 Separate the facial tissue into two layers (you need only one). Turn over the photocopy paper. Place the facial tissue over the photocopy paper. Gently brush a little water over the tissue using clean water. Wet the tissue all over, but do not saturate otherwise the raw sienna may show through.

4 Dilute white and black acrylic paint with water to make a very light gray. Paint the mixture over the tissue. Create thin lines with black paint. Blend the black lines with white paint. The overall effect should resemble birch bark. Allow to dry thoroughly.

5 Trace a 1½in (3.8cm) circle on the 'bark' and cut out. Using a pair of scissors, cut out four triangles each about ¼in (0.5cm) in depth, evenly spaced around the edge of the circle (see Fig 1.1).

6 Fold the edges of the triangles toward each other and overlap (see Fig 1.2). The 'bark' should form the exterior, the dark painted side the interior (see Fig 1.3). Apply a small amount of glue along the edges to secure, and trim the top if necessary to neaten.

7 Apply a thin line of glue along the top outside edge of the basket, and attach the light brown floss to form the rim. Repeat on the top inside edge.

8 Using a very fine sewing needle and dark brown thread, whipstitch along the top of the basket (see main photo).

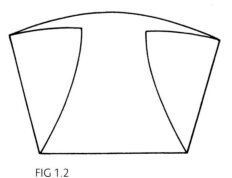

FIG 1.2

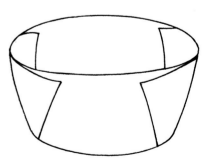

FIG 1.3

Reed basket

Reed baskets were made by 'coiling', a method more akin to sewing than weaving.

The basketmaker started the basket by winding a coil of dried fibers, usually cornhusks, yucca or long grasses. This first coil formed the center of the basket bottom. The basketmaker continued coiling the fibers in layers and stitched them to one another to form an increasingly larger coiled basket bottom until he or she achieved the desired size.

Although most North American tribes practised the art of coiled basketry, the Southwest tribes took it to an advanced level. Many of the tribes – the Hopis, Pimas, Apaches and Navajos – still make these baskets today. Some are made for tribal use and others are sold to tourists.

Create this miniature reed basket as an accessory for a Southwestern scene.

Tools and materials

Raffia (natural)
Scissors
Small bowl with water
Sewing needle
Paper towel

METHOD

1   Cut two to four lengths of raffia, each about 2ft (60cm) in length. Soften them in a bowl of water for approximately 30 minutes. Cut additional lengths, 1ft (30cm) long, to make the coils.

2   Squeeze out the excess water and pat dry with a paper towel. Flatten the raffia. Gently tear it into strips approximately ¼in (0.5cm) wide to create 'thread'. Set them aside to dry.

Finished size
1⅛in (3cm) high and 1⅛in (3cm) in diameter

3   Thread a needle with one of the 2ft (60cm) lengths of raffia. Take a 1ft (30cm) length of raffia and fold over one end. Wrap the raffia around the end to create a loop. Bring the thread up through the bottom of the loop and around the top six to eight times to fill in (see Figs 1.4A and B, overleaf). Clip ends to neaten.

4   Insert the raffia-threaded needle into the center of the coil, and wind the thread around the coil, creating continuous raffia layers.

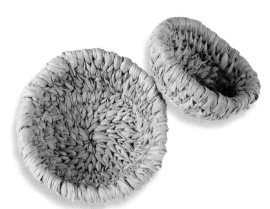

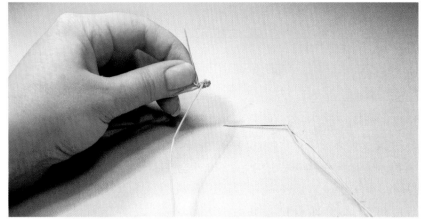

FIG 1.4A

FIG 1.4B

Keep the stitches close and even. Add more raffia as required. The bottom of the basket should consist of five or six rounds (see Figs 1.5A and B). Once the bottom is complete, begin stacking the coils to build up the sides of the basket.

5 To finish, wrap overlapping stitches around the top coil of the basket. Use a needle to string through the final few inches of raffia. Trim any loose ends.

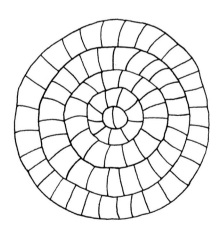

FIG 1.5A

FIG 1.5B

Trade beads

When Peter Minuit, the Dutch governor of the colony of New Netherland, legalized the colonization of the island of Manhattan by the Dutch West India Company in 1626, he had to find a way to reimburse the Native Americans who lived there for their land.

The Indians, most likely Algonquin, received cloth, trinkets and trade beads worth about 60 Dutch guilders (approximately $24) for a piece of land that today is priceless. It was renamed New Amsterdam and became the center of the company's trading and colonizing activities.

The deal for Manhattan was just one of many that the settlers and traders made with the Native Americans. Since there was no standard currency, many of the arrangements were made using trade beads, cloth and other items the tribes utilized.

Stringing the miniature beads with craft wire rather than thread will allow them to fall more naturally and make threading very easy. Make several strands at once and display them in a Native American setting or shop that sells Indian goods.

Tools and materials

Seed beads (muted, natural colors)
Craft wire
Wire cutter
Needle-nose pliers

METHOD

1 Cut a length of wire 3in (7.6cm) long. Thread the beads on the wire, selecting the colours at random.

2 Once you have threaded approximately three-quarters of the wire, twist the remaining length together with the pliers. Clip the wire close with the wire cutter. Fold the twist over. Slide a bead over the twist to disguise it.

Finished size

The threaded beads vary in size depending on the length of wire available, and the desired effect

Dream catcher

Tools and materials

Cloth-covered wire (floral wire)

Acrylic paint (brown)

Thread

One seed bead

Feathers, leather, twigs, beads
 for decoration (optional)

Wire cutters

Paintbrush

Needle

Small scissors

Tacky glue

Native Americans believe that dreams are a way of reaching the spirit world. Dreams can predict the future, warn the dreamer of impending trouble and help to make decisions.

A dream catcher is a tool the Native Americans use to capture dreams. A small circle made from red or yellow willow twigs forms the frame. The circle contains a woven web that catches the dreamer's good and bad dreams. The web even captures those dreams that the dreamer cannot remember. Feathers, beads or stones are attached to the circle. Their function is to help to make impossible dreams come true. They also represent the four seasons and points of the compass: north, south, east and west.

The dream catcher is hung by the bed or near a window. At first light, any bad dreams caught in the web disappear through a hole in the center and the good dreams travel down the feathers to become part of the dreamer's consciousness. Every dream catcher is unique, just like the dreamer who creates it.

Create a miniature dream catcher for your special scene.

Finished size

Approximately ¾in (2cm)
 in diameter

METHOD

1 Bend the piece of wire into a hoop, approximately ¾in (2cm) in diameter. Secure the hoop by wrapping thread several times around the ends. Apply a dab of glue to secure. Trim the thread ends. Cut the wire close on each end.

2 Paint the hoop with brown acrylic paint (dilute with a little water if necessary). Set aside to dry.

3 Thread a needle with thread, 2–3ft (60–90cm) long, but without knotting the end. To secure, tie a knot around the hoop where the ends meet.

4 To create the stitches you need, first form a loop by passing the needle over the hoop from front to back and up from the back (see Fig 1.6). Finish the stitch by passing the needle through the loop and pulling it taut. Continue the stitches in a clockwise direction around the hoop, forming them all in the same way. Space the stitches evenly, about every ¼in (0.5cm).

5 For the second and following rounds, use the stitches made in the first round, rather than the hoop to work new stitches, continuing toward the center.

6 On the third or fourth round, string a seed bead onto the needle to represent the spider in the web (see Fig 1.7). Continue making stitches. Near the center make a knot to secure. Do not forget to leave a hole for the bad dreams to fall through.

7 Leave a length of thread to attach feathers, beads or other decorations you may want to add.

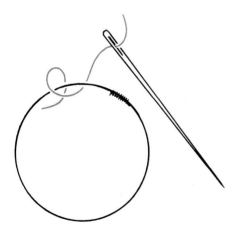

FIG 1.6

FIG 1.7

Wrapped feather

Tools and materials

Several small real feathers
Scrap of thin leather or suede
Silk or cotton thread
Seed bead (optional)
Small, fine scissors
PVA glue

Native Americans are very eco-friendly, only making use of the natural resources that they need to survive. To squander even the smallest flora, fauna, bird or insect was considered disrespectful of the bounty Nature offered and likely to result in bad luck.

A wrapped bird feather was used both as a ceremonial and a decorative object. It was added to a dream catcher or an 'ojo de dios' (God's eye), but also incorporated into tribal rituals, too.

Finished size

Approximately 1³⁄₈in (3.5cm) in length

METHOD

1 Take a single feather and cut it ³⁄₄in (2cm) back from the tip with a pair of fine scissors.

2 Trim the feather further by cutting along the vein ³⁄₄in (2cm) from the bottom (see Fig 1.8).

3 Cut away a little down from a few of the feathers and stack onto the front of one of the trimmed feathers. Slide a seed bead up the vein to the base of the gathered feather down.

4 Cut a piece of thin leather or suede ¹⁄₂ x ¹⁄₄in (1.25 x 0.5cm) wide. Wrap it around the base of the feather and secure with a dab of glue.

5 Wrap thread tightly five or six times around the feather near the end. Secure with a dab of glue.

FIG 1.8

God's eye

The Huichol Indians of Mexico believed that the God's eye or 'ojo de dios' symbol offered healing and protective powers. They wove a God's eye to invoke spiritual protection over a newborn child while it slept. It was also used for ceremonial purposes.

When a child was born, the father wove one color of thread around two sticks to form a cross: this created the center of the eye. Tradition has it that an additional eye is added to the original weaving for every year thereafter until the child reaches the age of five. Many children did not live to reach their first birthday, so five signaled the promise of a long, full life.

Each color symbolized something different: yellow represented the sun, moon and stars, blue meant the sky and water, brown signified the soil, green symbolized vegetation, and black meant death.

For the Huichol, the cross represented the four elements: earth, fire, water and air, different from the Christian symbol of Christ on the cross. Like the Huichol, the peoples of Tibet and Chile weave similar symbols for spiritual protection.

Tools and materials

Two sticks, $^3/_{32}$ x 1$^3/_4$in (0.2 x 4.5cm) long
Thread (various colors)
Wrapped feathers (optional)
Scissors
PVA glue
Square

Finished size

1$^3/_4$in (4.5cm) square

METHOD

1 Glue the two sticks together in the center to form a cross. Make sure that the cross is perfectly square (see Fig 1.9).

2 To weave your threads, tie on the first colored thread to the cross and knot the thread at the back. Follow Fig 1.10, overleaf, for guidance on weaving the thread around the sticks. Keep the threads taut.

FIG 1.9

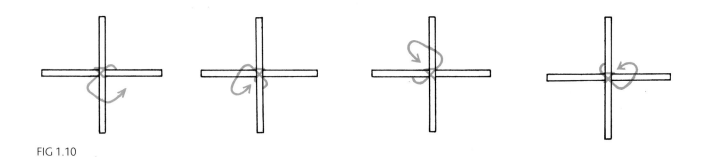

FIG 1.10

3 Tie off the colored thread on the back of one of the sticks. Tie on the second colored thread, making sure the knots do not show from the front, or use a dab of glue to secure. Continue with this method of weaving to within ⅛–¼in (0.25–0.5cm) from the edges. See Figs 1.11 and 1.12 below for guidance on how the front and back should look as you work.

4 Decorate your completed God's eye with wrapped feathers, beads or other items, or leave it unadorned if you wish.

FIG 1.11

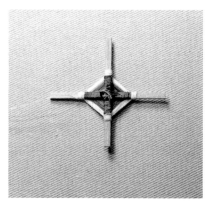

FIG 1.12

Cornhusk doll

The cornhusk doll originates with the early Native Americans. Mothers would make them to amuse their children. The Iroquois tribe also incorporated them into their ritual ceremonies.

Corn was a staple of the Native American way of life. They used every part of the plant: for food, clothing, medicine, household utensils and decorative objects. The husk was transformed into sleeping mats, thatched roofs, moccasins, masks, baskets and dolls.

The best husks are obtained when the corn is ripe and beginning to dry on the stalk. Cornhusk dolls can be made from green husks and will keep their color if dried in the shade. If dried in the sun, they turn pale tan.

Husks can be shaped into any form when wet. They hold their shape as they dry, which makes them easy to work.

A Native American myth describes how, many years ago, the cornhusk dolls had faces. But one pretty doll came across her reflection in a pool of water. Instead of continuing her work, she became vain and caused disruption among the other cornhusk people. As punishment, the Great Spirit removed her face and forbade cornhusk people to ever have them again.

Whether you make your miniature doll with real cornhusks or from raffia, it will add an ethnic touch to a Native American scene. And, if you dare to defy the Great Spirit, you may wish to add faces to some of them.

Tools and materials
Raffia (natural)
Matching thread
Scissors
Small bowl with water

Finished size
1¹⁄₄in (3.2cm) high

METHOD

1 Cut five to six strands of raffia into 6¹⁄₂in (16.5cm) lengths. Soak the strands in water until pliable (about 30 minutes).

2 Uncurl one of the raffia strands. Gently pull apart the strand, splitting it into ¹⁄₄in (0.5cm) strips.

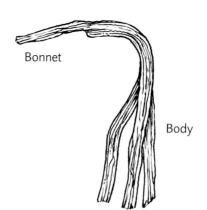

Bonnet

Body

FIG 1.13

FIG 1.14

FIG 1.15

3 Fold one of the ¼in (0.5cm) strips in half three times to make a bundle ¾in (2cm) long. Using another ¼in (0.5cm) strip, tightly wrap it around the bundle to form the arms. Tuck the ends into the folds to secure (see Fig 1.13).

4 Uncurl three more raffia strands. Gently pull apart the strands, splitting them into ½in (1.25cm) strips.

5 Place five ½in (1.25cm) strips on top of each other. Fold them in half twice, then fold this in half lengthwise.

6 Place one ½in (1.25cm) strip over the folded end to form the doll's 'bonnet' (see Fig 1.14).

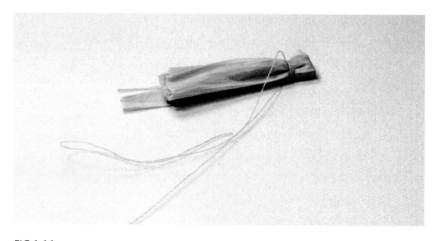

FIG 1.16

FIG 1.17

FIG 1.18

7 Pinch the raffia together near the top. Tightly tie a piece of thread ¹⁄₄in (0.5cm) down from the top to form the head (see Figs 1.15 and 1.16) and trim the thread.

8 Place the arms on the body just below the head. Tie a piece of thread below the arms (see Fig 1.17) and trim the thread.

9 Fold a ¹⁄₂in (1.25cm) strip of raffia in half lengthwise. This piece represents the shawl. Wrap it around the shoulders and cross it over at the front (see Fig 1.18).

10 Tear a length of raffia, about ¹⁄₁₆in (0.2cm) thick, for apron strings. Cut a ¹⁄₄in (0.5cm) wide strip of raffia, 1in (2.5cm) in length. Fold the ¹⁄₄in (0.5cm) strip in half over the top of the ¹⁄₁₆in (0.2cm) strip to create an apron (see Fig 1.19). Tie the apron around the waist of the doll. Trim the raffia string.

11 Trim the bottom of the doll so that it stands approximately 1¹⁄₄in (3.2cm) tall. The raffia will curl slightly as it dries.

FIG 1.19

Moccasins

Tools and materials

Soft, thin piece of leather

Matching thread

Photocopy paper (white)

Fine sewing needle

Scissors

Toothpick

Tweezers

Non-permanent (stick) glue

Moccasins were the preferred footwear for most Native American tribes, with the exception of those in the Southwest and Mexico who wore sandals.

The word 'moccasin' is an Algonquin word that describes footwear made with a single piece of soft animal hide: often deerskin, but sometimes buffalo or salmon skins. The hide is folded from the bottom of the foot at the sole and over the toes to the ankle, and secured with a back seam and a few stitches on top. Using this design, tribes developed several distinct styles, modifying them to suit their own climate and terrain. Some were lined with fur, and others incorporated a second sole for added wear-and-tear.

Native Americans often decorated the tops of their moccasins with beads; they believed that feet should be as beautiful as the flowers and grass they walked on. Moccasins with heavily beaded soles were used as burial moccasins.

Moccasin design was proprietary to a particular tribe. To wear the moccasins of another meant giving up the customs and laws of one's own tribe.

The Woodland Indians, whose terrain was covered in pine needles, leaves and soft grass, wore the soft-soled buckskin Woodland-style moccasins upon which our project is based.

For this project, use the thinnest, softest leather you can find. An old driving glove will provide enough leather for these moccasins as well as many other projects.

Finished size

Each moccasin is $^7/_8$in (2.2cm) in length

METHOD

1 Trace the moccasin pattern onto a piece of photocopy paper (see Fig 1.20). You will need two patterns for each pair of moccasins. Trim around the pattern. Apply the pattern to the wrong side of the leather with nonpermanent glue (see Fig 1.21). With a sharp pair of scissors, cut out the moccasins following the solid lines.

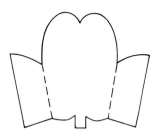

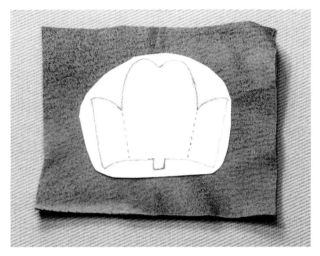

FIG 1.20

FIG 1.21

2 Peel off the patterns from the leather. Fold each moccasin in half with right sides together. Following Fig 1.22, sew tiny stitches very close to the edges, from the tip of the toe (A) to the beginning of the flap (B), using a fine needle and matching thread. Knot the thread. Trim close.

3 Make sure the flap is turned to the inside of the moccasins. Sew from the bottom back of the moccasins to the top (C to D). Knot the thread and trim close (see Fig 1.23).

4 Turn the moccasins right side out, using the tip of a toothpick to push out the toe. Pull out the back flap with tweezers. Fold over the flaps on each side using the dotted line as a guide (see Fig 1.20). Tack in place, if necessary. Insert a small scrap of leather into each toe to maintain the moccasin shape.

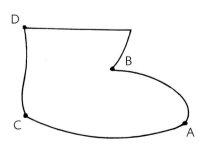

FIG 1.22

FIG 1.23

Southwest sun faces

Tools and materials

Polymer clay (eg. Sculpey)
(white)

Acrylic paint (terracotta)

Bamboo skewer and small
amount of polymer clay
(to make a tool)

Craft knife

Toothpick

Oven

Ceramic tile or several sheets of
aluminum foil

Paintbrush

Circular template

Flour (optional)

Finished size

1¹/₂in (3.8cm) in diameter

These enduringly popular ornamental sun faces may have originated in Metepec, Mexico. Located near Mexico City and the famous market of Toluca, Metepec is home to potters who have made mythical clay figures for hundreds of years. The Museo Anthropologico Nacional (Museum of National Anthropology) exhibits a clay toy from this region that dates back to AD 650.

Since the nineteenth century, potters have sold clay statues representing saints and other religious figures to families for use in Christmas crèches. The statues are also used as icons for religious offerings.

From the religious pieces, it was a small step for potters to mold clay into secular objects for the tourists that frequented the Toluca market. Some of these objects included peacocks and mythical creatures.

To make a piece, the potter would choose a design and make a mold. The sun symbol, with its emphasis on life and light, was a popular design. The clay was pressed over the mold and allowed to dry. The resulting figure was removed and allowed to dry in the sun for several days, then fired in a kiln.

Although many Metepec figures are painted in vivid colors, some are left as unadorned terracotta.

METHOD

1 First create a tool for manipulating the clay. To do this, place a small amount of polymer clay on the pointed end of a bamboo skewer or small dowel, and bake according to the manufacturer's instructions.

2 Make three balls of polymer clay: two ³/₈in (1cm) in diameter, one ¹/₂in (1.25cm) in diameter (see Fig 1.24).

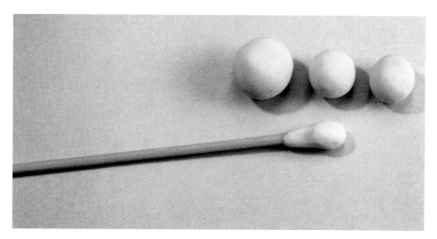

FIG 1.24

3 Flatten the $\frac{1}{2}$in (1.25cm) ball to a diameter of $1\frac{1}{4}$in (3.2cm) and $\frac{1}{16}$in (0.1cm) thick by pressing it on a ceramic tile.

FIG 1.25

4 Cut one of the $\frac{3}{8}$in (1cm) balls in half by rolling the craft knife through the middle. Place one half in the center of the flattened ball.

5 Flatten the other $\frac{3}{8}$in (1cm) ball to a diameter of $\frac{3}{4}$in (2cm) and $\frac{1}{16}$in (0.1cm) thick on the ceramic tile. Place this piece over the half ball and smooth the edges with the clay tool you have made (see Figs 1.25 and 1.26).

FIG 1.26

6 Form the sun's eyes, eyebrows and mouth with a toothpick or other sharp-pointed tool. (You may want to practise first.)

7 For the nose, roll a very small piece of clay into a rope, slightly tapered at one end. The clay rope should reach from the base of the eyebrows to the top of the mouth. Smooth the edges and form into shape.

8 Place the $\frac{3}{4}$in (2cm) hole of the circular template over the center of the sun. Press lightly to form a ridge. Use the ridge as a guide.

9 **Option 1** Cut out evenly spaced V shapes around the sun with a craft knife to represent the rays (see Fig 1.27).

FIG 1.27

FIG 1.28

9 **Option 2** Press a toothpick into the clay to make indentations, not cuts (see Fig 1.28). The tip of the toothpick should just touch the ridge. Repeat the process so that the marks are evenly spaced around the sun. If the toothpick sticks, dragging the clay, dip it in flour which helps to make a clean mark.

10 Bake the sun faces according to manufacturer's instructions and set aside to cool. Once done, neaten the edges with a sharp craft knife if necessary.

11 Paint the faces with two coats of terracotta acrylic paint (diluted with water if necessary), allowing the faces to dry completely between coats. Note how the features really stand out.

Pueblo storyteller

Storytelling is an ancient art, and one that is used to pass on traditions and communicate the past. Native American elders used storytelling as a way to explain to its youth the tribe's origins and ways of life.

At a time when there was no written language, passing information orally from one generation to another was critical to the survival of a tribe's accumulated knowledge.

The Pueblos were one such tribe who relied on storytellers for information dissemination. They are descendants of an ancient people inhabiting the 'Four Corners' region, the point at which the boundaries of Arizona, Utah, New Mexico and Colorado conjoin.

For centuries, the Pueblo peoples have made clay figurines to resemble humans, but in 1964, Helen Cordero, a Pueblo artist from the Cochiti tribe of New Mexico, created a special clay figure to honor the important work of the storyteller. This figure featured a seated woman with captivated children gathered about her arms and lap.

Each storyteller is unique. Potters create distinctive male and female figures to honor favorite relatives. Some display great character and emotion.

To create a storyteller, potters first dig clay from the ground and, to strengthen, soak it in water and mix with sand. Once combined, the clay figure is formed, left to dry and then sanded until smooth. It is then coated in 'slip', a thin dilution of clay and water. The resulting surface is polished with special stones and painted with paint made from diluted clay. A plant called Rocky Mountain beeweed is boiled to make 'guaco', an inky black liquid, which is used to decorate the piece. Finally, it is fired in a kiln. If the piece cracks at any time, the potter must return the clay to the earth and begin again.

Make a miniature Pueblo storyteller to display in a gift shop or as an accessory on a miniature collector's shelf.

Tools and materials

Polymer clay (eg. Sculpey) (white)
Acrylic paint (antique white, terracotta, black)
Paintbrushes of various sizes, including fine-tipped
Oven
Ceramic tile or several sheets of aluminum foil
Dressmaker's pin
Tacky glue

Finished size
⁷/₈in (2.2cm) high

METHOD

1 Roll a ½in (1.25cm) piece of polymer clay into a rope, 2in (5cm) long and ⅛in (0.25cm) thick. Place the rope on a ceramic tile or a couple of layers of aluminum foil. Fold the rope in half to make a U shape. Bend each end upward slightly to form the feet (see Fig 1.29).

2 Roll a ball of polymer clay ⅜in (1cm) in diameter. Place the ball in the center of the U for the body (see Fig 1.30). Press the body gently into place.

3 Roll a ¼in (0.5cm) piece of polymer clay into a rope about 1¼ x ³⁄₃₂in (3.2 x 0.2cm) for the arms. Fold the rope into a U shape. Place the rope on top of the body. Bend the arms to rest gently on the knees (see Fig 1.31).

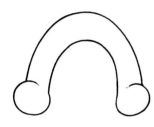

FIG 1.29

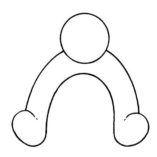

FIG 1.30

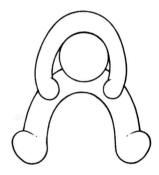

FIG 1.31

4 For the head, form a small ball of clay approximately ¼in (0.5cm) in diameter. Roll another very small ball of clay. Place it toward the top of the head for the nose. Gently place the nose onto the head (see Fig 1.32).

5 Form another ball for the hair. Place it on the back of the head, slightly below center. Flatten the ball a little to resemble a bun.

6 To form the mouth, pierce the head using the point of a dressmaker's pin. Wiggle the pin slightly to widen the hole into an O shape.

7 Place the head on top of the arms and press gently. The head should be tilted back slightly.

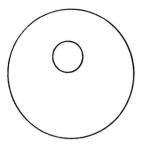

FIG 1.32

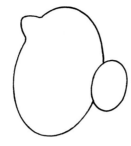

FIG 1.33

FIG 1.34

8 Make four or five children to sit on the storyteller. For each child, form a small rope of clay, $\frac{1}{4}$ x $\frac{1}{16}$in (0.5 x 0.1cm) thick. Bend the rope slightly to form arms. For the head, make a small ball and place it in the center of the U. Make another rope $\frac{1}{4}$ x $\frac{1}{16}$in (0.5 x 0.1cm) thick. For the legs, bend the rope into a U. Place the legs on the bottom of the arms (see Fig 1.34). Lightly place each child on the lap and arms of the storyteller. Bend the limbs into place and remove: the children are baked separately and attached once painted.

9 Bake according to the manufacturer's instructions and, once hardened, leave to cool.

10 Paint the storyteller and children with a creamy white acrylic paint to resemble 'slip'.

11 Using a fine-tipped paintbrush, paint the hair on the storyteller and children with black acrylic paint. Decorate the shirts and pants of the children and the storyteller with terracotta and black paint.

12 Paint closed eyes on the storyteller with a very fine-tipped paintbrush, then paint eyes and mouths on the children with black paint.

13 Mix a dab of terracotta acrylic paint with some creamy white. Paint the bottom of the storyteller's feet.

14 Once the paint is dry, apply glue with the tip of the pin to the children's behinds and secure them into position.

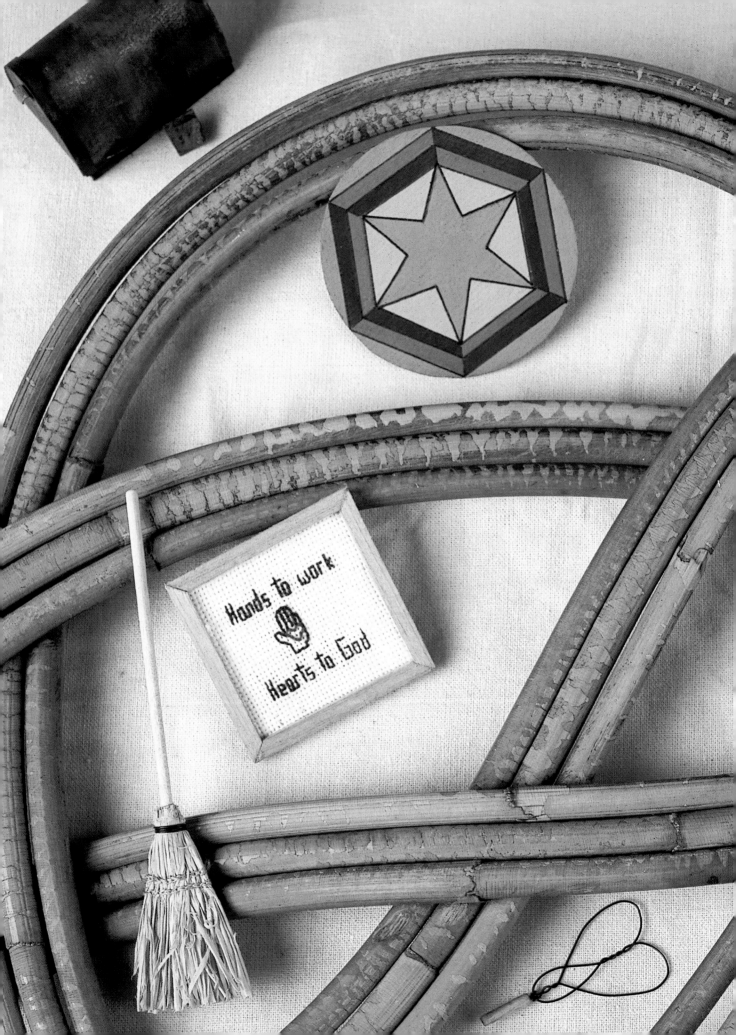

Rural

Stick shuttle ⭐ Hex sign

Popcorn and cranberry chains ⭐ Shaker box

Pumpkin pie ⭐ Shaker sampler

Rug beater ⭐ Shaker flat broom

Rag rug ⭐ Checkerboard and checkers

Mailbox ⭐ Shoo-fly quilt

The long-running TV show, *Little House on the Prairie,* was based on the memoirs of Laura Ingalls Wilder, a young woman who grew up in rural America in the nineteenth century. The show attempted to convey the experiences of those living in rural communities during this period.

During the nineteenth century, the primary motivator for the westward migration across America was the Homestead Act of 1862. Any man who farmed 160 acres of unclaimed land could then claim the land for his own. This meant that ranchers, whose cows grazed the land, had no claim to it.

Land was the chief form of wealth in the US, and farms were passed down from fathers to eldest sons. The offer of 160 acres of free land with no strings attached was too good for many to resist. Armed with the desire to be self-sufficient, many pioneers chose to escape the cities for the wide-open prairies.

Farming was the principal occupation of these settlers. Families grew their own vegetables and reared their own livestock. In 1850, the average family raised enough food to feed four families. (Today's farmer feeds almost 20 times as many.)

Hard work was a given, but the farmers' success depended heavily on the cooperation of Mother Nature. Many crops were ruined by early frosts, infestations of bugs or drought.

The migration west across America to claim land

The invasion of the Oregon country – settlers landing their goods from a river steamboat, circa 1900

Even on the prairie, farmers' children received an education. Families joined forces to build a one-room schoolhouse and hire a teacher – generally an unmarried woman, but sometimes also a man – to teach all ages and abilities. At planting or harvest time, however, most children were obliged to forgo school to help their families in the fields. The single-room schoolhouse often became the hub of local activities such as political elections, holiday celebrations and town meetings.

Today's rural pioneers are quite different. They are no longer interested in farming or exploring uncharted territories, but want to 'get back to the land' or escape the stress of urban life. They see country living as a way of simplifying their lives.

Stick shuttle

Tools and materials

Strip basswood, $^5/_{32}$ x 1$^1/_2$in
(0.3 x 3.8cm)
Cotton thread (various colors)
Extra-fine grade sandpaper
Craft knife with a sharp blade
Round needle-nose file
(optional)
Tacky glue

Stick shuttles are smooth, flat sticks with notched ends used to wind the warp or lengthwise threads onto a loom. They are also used to pass the threads back and forth during the weaving process. Warp or weft materials such as carpet thread or rags can be wound on the shuttle using a figure-eight pattern, which makes the shuttle flatter for easier weaving.

Stick shuttles are made in different lengths depending upon the width of the item. When used for weft materials, a variety of pre-wound shuttles makes the weaving go more quickly.

Wind several miniature shuttles with different-colored thread and place them in a miniature basket in a country home or next to a loom.

METHOD

1 Cut the basswood to length and sand smooth. Run sandpaper along the edges at an angle to slightly round off the long edges.

2 Cut a small V or notch into each end of the stick with a craft knife (see Fig 2.1).

Finished size
$^5/_{32}$ x 1$^1/_2$in (0.3 x 3.8cm)

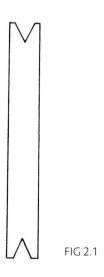

FIG 2.1

FIG 2.2

3 Round off the base of the V with the round file. Alternatively, use a piece of extra-fine sandpaper.

4 To wind the thread on the shuttle, start with the end of the thread at the back, then bring it to the front of the shuttle over the top. Wind it using a figure-eight motion along one side, about 15 times (see Fig 2.2). Switch sides. Continue winding along the other side, again 15 times, then down the middle of the shuttle 15 times. Bring the thread to the back of the shuttle and secure with a small dab of glue.

Hex sign

The Pennsylvania Dutch (or more accurately 'Deutsch': the Germans) settled in southeastern Pennsylvania in the late 1600s. Most of the settlers were peasant farmers who migrated there seeking the religious freedom offered by William Penn, after whom the state was named.

The Amish and Mennonite settlers were called 'plain', and Lutherans and other more worldly Reformed groups were called 'fancy'. Because of religious and political persecution in their homelands, the settlers kept to themselves and shunned modern life. Instead, they worked hard to create fine crafts and develop one of the best farming regions in America.

The hex sign originated in the mid-1800s when the 'fancy' farmers began painting these geometric signs on their distinctive red barns, perhaps to ward off evil or to signify cultural pride.

The designs were enclosed within a circle for symmetry. While many are geometric, they also include flowers, birds and heart motifs. Modern examples include words: 'welcome', 'love', or family names.

The symbols had specific meanings: a sun wheel means warmth and fertility; hearts for love; birds (especially goldfinches, or 'distelfinks') for good luck and happiness; tulips for faith and

Tools and materials
Piece of thin 3in (7.6cm)
  square cardboard
Acrylic paint (own colors)
Pencil
Fine-tipped permanent
  marker (black)
Compass or circular template
Scissors
Paintbrush
Metal straight-edged ruler

stars for luck. Colors also had significance, often of a religious nature: red represented emotions; yellow for love of man, and the sun; green for growth; blue for protection; white for purity and brown for the earth.

Historians disagree over the origin of the word 'hex', but most likely it originates with 'hexagon': the six-pointed star, upon which many designs are based.

Create several of your own hex signs, using different colours, motifs and names, to hang on the outside of your miniature barn.

METHOD

1 Cut a 2in (5cm) diameter circle from a piece of cardboard. Any plain scrap piece will do.

2 Paint the front and back of the cardboard circle with acrylic paint in a light color: the sample uses beige. Allow the paint to dry thoroughly.

3 Draw the geometric pattern onto the cardboard – or create your own design.

4 Paint the other colors, following the pattern (see main photo, previous page, or Fig 2.3). Allow each color to dry thoroughly before painting the next.

5 Outline the design with a pencil or a very fine-tipped permanent marker and a metal ruler.

Finished size

2in (5cm) in diameter

FIG 2.3

Popcorn and cranberries

Believe it or not, popcorn has been around for over 5,000 years. The oldest ears of popcorn were discovered in the Bat Cave, west central New Mexico, in 1948.

Some Native American tribes harvested corn specifically for popping. Others, such as the Aztecs, used popcorn in their rituals. They would create ceremonial headdresses and other ornaments from the popped corn and place them on the statues of their gods. It found its way to the pilgrims' Thanksgiving table in the form of a gift from Wampanoag tribesman, Quadequina, upon their arrival in the New World.

Present-day popped corn cereal can be traced back to colonial times when popcorn was served with milk and sugar. Hot molasses poured over popcorn and rolled between greased palms was a Christmas treat.

During the Depression, even people of limited means could afford to eat popcorn. It was one of the few businesses that flourished during this era. It also satisfied the cravings of Americans during World War II when sugar rationing limited candy production.

Popcorn sales took a dip during the 1950s, in part due to the advent of television: people had always eaten popcorn at the movies. Sales enjoyed a resurgence when Americans began eating it again while watching their favorite TV shows. It has continued to rise in popularity ever since: the Popcorn Board reveals that pre-packed microwave popcorn accounted for over $240 million in US popcorn sales during the 1990s.

Each popcorn kernel is composed of a drop of water contained by a layer of soft starch and encased in a hard shell. When heated, the water turns to steam, which applies pressure and causes it to explode. Kernels lacking sufficient moisture remain unpopped. Rather unkindly, these were once referred to as 'old maids', but are now referred to as 'duds': the slang term for unexploded bombs.

The cranberry is truly an all-American food. When the pilgrims arrived at Plymouth, Massachusetts in 1620, the cranberry was the only fruit that they could harvest. This is probably because it thrives even in poor and acidic soil.

The tart, red fruit was a staple of the Native Americans' diet. They were accustomed to eating it fresh or dried so it is not surprising that the berry found its way onto the menu of the settlers' first Thanksgiving.

The name of the fruit comes from the Latin *vaccinium* which translates as 'cow plant'. Cows found the plant's foliage a delicious treat.

Cranberries contain a natural preservative called benzoic acid which allows the fruit to keep well without cooking, drying or freezing. Because of this ability, the berries were often carried on long sea voyages, stored in barrels of water until required. Cranberries are also an excellent source of antioxidants and vitamins and are effective in preventing different infections.

Popcorn and cranberry chains

Most likely taking their cue from the Native Americans, the colonists began threading kernels of popped corn to form chains, which they hung in their homes for decoration.

German Lutheran settlers created the first authentic American Christmas tree ornament by stringing chains of popcorn and hanging them on the tree branches. It was a simple step to add colorful, shiny cranberries to the white popped kernels for a festive decoration.

String your own miniature popcorn and cranberry chains, or fill miniature bowls with popcorn and cranberries to show the work in progress.

METHOD

1 Separate pieces of Styrofoam to make the popcorn. Shape them into popped kernels by pinching with your fingernails. Add centers by dabbing the kernels with dark brown acrylic paint.

2 Form a puddle of each of the red acrylic paints in separate parts of a piece of wax paper. Make a third puddle by combining the two reds. Mix a few drops of glue into each of the three paint puddles. Add a teaspoon or so of the mustard seeds to the mixtures. Roll the seeds around to coat them, then separate each one using a toothpick. Spread them out evenly on the wax paper to dry and put to one side.

3 Once dry, thread the popcorn and cranberries to form a chain. Use a very fine, sharp needle for this task or else they will split.

Tools and materials

Bead-style Styrofoam

Mustard seeds

Acrylic paint (raspberry red, cranberry red and dark brown)

Toothpick

Thread (ecru)

Scissors

Fine small-eyed needle

PVA glue

Wax paper

Finished size

The popcorn and cranberry chains can vary in length as desired

The Shakers

'Tis a gift to be simple' begins a traditional Shaker song. The lyric describes the philosophy of the Shakers, a group of English dissidents from the Anglican Church. Ann Lee, an illiterate preacher, assumed spiritual leadership for a small flock of believers she brought to America in the late eighteenth century. Mother Lee and her followers emigrated to seek religious freedom, and settled in small communities from Maine to Kentucky.

The Shaker name came from the term 'Shaking Quakers', so-called because individuals, filled with the Holy Spirit, shook during worship.

The Shakers were famous for their simple way of living which was also, effectively, a rejection of the outside world. But despite this, Shaker society was egalitarian. Everyone was considered equal, and each member had his or her own duties. The Shakers believed that doing everyday things as perfectly as possible was a way of honoring God, who saw everything they did, including their work.

The Shakers strove for self-sufficiency and rejected modern inventions. Shaker craftsmen and women made many everyday items, which were characterized by simple, flawless designs. To help them make a living, they sold many of these high-quality items to the general public.

As America's best-known communal utopian society, the Shakers once numbered 6,000. However, the arrival of the twentieth century saw the settlements begin to disappear, one by one, as their members died without being replaced by new recruits. Today, the only remaining Shaker settlement is located in Sabbathday Lake, Maine, and numbers just six people.

Shaker box

Shaker boxes were made from wood, usually maple, which was steamed and molded into a round or oval shape. Characteristic of these boxes are the 'swallow tails' cut into one end of a length of wood and overlapped and secured to the other end with copper or wrought iron rivets. The base and lid were cut from pine.

The boxes were made to fit inside each other, and frequently sold as sets. Some designs included handles or were painted to increase their commercial appeal.

Make a set of miniature boxes to stack next to a rocking chair, or for storage.

Tools and materials
Card

Acrylic paint (sandstone and copper)

Stencil cream paint (warm brown)

Four or five coins, about the size of a quarter or ten-pence piece

Ruler

Craft knife

Soft paintbrush

Dressmaker's pins

Scissors

Mechanical or sharp, fine pencil

Metal straight-edged ruler

Square

Tacky glue

Cotton swab, or bud

METHOD

1 Using the coin as a guide for size, draw around it twice onto a piece of card with a sharp pencil. Lightly mark one of the circles with a T (for top) and the other with a B (for bottom).

2 Cut the circle marked with a T on the outside of the line. Cut the one marked with a B on the inside of the line. This is to ensure a good fit. Set aside.

3 Transfer the side templates to a piece of card and carefully cut out, following the lines (see Fig 2.4).

Finished size
1 x ¹/₂in (2.5 x 1.25cm)

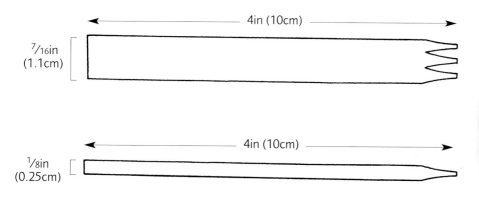

4in (10cm)

⁷/₁₆in (1.1cm)

4in (10cm)

¹/₈in (0.25cm)

FIG 2.4

53

4 Dry-fit the $^7/_{16}$in (1.1cm) strip around a stack of coins. Line up the ends so that the swallow tails overlap by $^1/_8$in (0.25cm). Make a mark where this occurs, and trim.

5 Place the circle marked with a B on top of the stack of coins. Dry-fit the strip around the coins. Hold together for a moment, then remove the strip. Use the needle to place a fine line of glue around the circle of card. Press the strip around the circle, starting with the cut end. When you reach the swallow tails, add a little glue to the underside. Press the swallow tails onto the strip. Hold in place for a few minutes to allow the glue to dry. Clean up any excess.

6 Repeat step 5 with the T-marked circle and the $^1/_8$in (0.25cm) strip, ensuring that the 'tails' end is facing the same way. Test-fit the top onto the bottom. The fit should be nice and secure.

7 Paint the box on the inside and outside with acrylic paint in sandstone and leave to dry.

8 Dip the cotton swab, or bud, into the dark brown stencil paint. Since this paint takes time to dry, you have time to get it right. Brush the inside of the box with the stencil paint and, once the inside is done, brush over it with a paintbrush to create a wood-grain effect. Allow the box to dry overnight. The following day, repeat the process on the outside and bottom of the box. Again, allow to dry overnight.

9 Once your box is dry, use the pin and the copper acrylic paint to simulate nail heads. Paint two nail heads on each tail and one on the box across from the tails (see Figs 2.5 and 2.6).

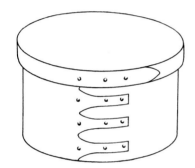

FIG 2.5

FIG 2.6

Pumpkin pie

A variation of pumpkin pie may also have featured at the first Thanksgiving feast. But even if it did not, the dessert has become an enduring favorite of the American Thanksgiving dinner.

The pumpkin is a vegetable native to North America. Pumpkin seeds have been found in Mexico dating back to 7000 BC. It grows on vines like its squash cousins. The name is thought to derive from old French: 'pompon'.

Pumpkins are not only grown for food. The early settlers believed that spirits rose from the grave on Halloween looking for shelter. They carved pumpkins into jack-o'-lanterns to ward against the spirits.

While the average pumpkin weighs between 15lb (6.8kg) and 30lb (13.6kg), some have exceeded 800lb (362kg). Annual competitions attract growers who can stake a claim for the largest vegetable. Pumpkin seeds (and the secrets of cultivation) are traded in the hope of producing an even larger specimen the following year.

The flesh of the pumpkin is eaten when fully ripe. Its rather bland taste is spiced up with cinnamon, ginger or nutmeg when cooked in a pie, and frequently topped with whipped cream. Pumpkin seeds can be salted and baked until dry for a nutritious crunchy snack.

Create a miniature pumpkin pie for your Thanksgiving scene or simply place one on a windowsill as though left to cool.

Tools and materials
Card
Plaster or water putty
Acrylic paint (silver and raw sienna)
Small, thin rubber band (beige)
Chalk or pastels (light and dark brown)
Hairspray
Scissors or craft knife
Paintbrush
Mixing cup, stick and water
PVA glue

METHOD

1 To make the miniature 8in pie tin, first cut a circle $1^1/_{16}$in (2.2cm) in diameter out of card. Within the first circle, draw a second circle $^3/_4$in (2cm) in diameter inside. Cut around the larger circle. Carefully cut out the smaller circle, then trim $^1/_4$in (0.5cm) off the larger circle.

Finished size
Approximately $1^1/_{16}$in (2.7cm) in diameter

2 For the base, cut another card circle $^5/_8$in (1.6cm) in diameter. Glue the ends of the outer circle together, overlapping the edge by $^1/_4$in (0.5cm). This will form the rim of the pie plate. Apply a little glue around the $^5/_8$in (1.6cm) circle. Drop the smaller circle in from the top, then press into the bottom of the pie plate. Allow to dry.

3 Paint the pie plate inside and out with silver acrylic paint and leave to dry.

4 Mix a small amount of plaster or water putty according to the manufacturer's directions. Add a drop or two of raw sienna paint to the mix. Fill the pie plate to within $^1/_8$in (0.25cm) of the rim.

5 For a realistic crust, cut the rubber band to fit along the inside edge of the pie plate before the plaster sets. Press it gently into place. Allow the plaster to dry.

6 Brush light and dark brown chalk on the rubber band to darken the colour, and on the center of the pie. Spray the finished pie lightly with hairspray to add a slight shine and to help set the chalk.

Shaker sampler

Believers in the adage that 'idle hands are the devil's playground', the Shakers pursued perfection in their work as part of their dedication to God. Mottos such as 'Hands to work and hearts to God' reminded them of their purpose in life.

Wall hangings served a dual function: a tangible reminder of their beliefs, and to help the walls of their rooms retain heat.

Mount this miniature sampler in a room box or dolls' house, or in a miniature gift shop.

METHOD

1 Work the cross-stitch pattern (see Fig 2.7) using a single strand of floss. Be careful not to pull the stitches too tightly.

2 Remove the fabric from the embroidery hoop and wash in cold water if soiled. Iron dry. Clip any long threads from the back.

3 Cut the fabric to 1½in (3.8cm) square. Cut a piece of cardboard the same size. Apply a thin layer of glue to the cardboard. Center the stitching over the cardboard. Press into place.

4 Use strip wood to create a simple frame. Miter the corners before assembling. Dry-fit the frame parts. Stain the frame, if desired. Apply the frame to the top of the stitching with glue. You can also use a ready-made frame or leave the sampler unframed.

Tools and materials

28-count cross-stitch fabric
Embroidery floss (dark blue, red, dark gray)
Backing material (eg. card)
Strip wood for frame
Wood stain (brown)
Scissors
Needle
Embroidery hoop
PVA glue

Finished size
1½in (3.8cm) square

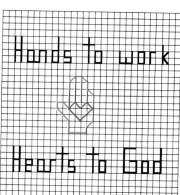

FIG 2.7

Rug beater

Tools and materials

28-gauge steel wire

$^1/_{16}$in (0.1cm) dowel, $^3/_8$in
  (1cm) long

Wire cutters

Needle-nose pliers

Pin or small drill

PVA glue

Finished size

Approximately $1^6/_{16}$ in (3.5cm)
  in length

Before the advent of carpet sweepers and vacuum cleaners in the early twentieth century, American housewives had fewer cleaning options for rugs and upholstery. If a rug was small enough, it could be washed or taken outside and vigorously shaken. Otherwise, it had to be hung over a washing line or fence and repeatedly struck with a rug beater. Many homes had a small upper floor called a 'maid's balcony', where small rugs were hung and beaten with a rug beater.

Carpets, rugs, upholstery cushions, quilts and bedspreads were all beaten with a rug beater to eliminate dust and dirt. Although the beatings were tough on the surface of the rug, they did not suck up fibers like vacuum cleaners do today, so the rug remained in good condition for much longer – sometimes many years – and many have become heirlooms and museum pieces.

Rug beaters were made from rattan, wicker or cane, but most commonly from metal or steel springs.

Hang a miniature rug beater on a peg on the wall of your country home, or lean it up against a fence or washing line with a rug over it.

METHOD

1 Cut a piece of wire 1ft (30cm) long. Holding the two ends, make a loop in the middle to create an elongated teardrop shape (see Fig 2.8). Twist the bottom of the teardrop three or four times to secure together. The total length of the drop and twist should be $^7/_8$in (2.2cm).

FIG 2.8

2 Invert the teardrop-shaped wire so that the largest part is facing downward. Curve the two wire ends around to form a heart shape (see Fig 2.9 or photo, facing opposite).

3 Twist the wires together at the base of the heart. Pull the sides of the heart upward to raise the twist inside the teardrop.

4 Wrap the wire ends around the base of the teardrop and twist them together tightly. Clip the wire close to the last twist leaving one wire end extended.

5 Make a hole in the center of the dowel handle with a small drill or pin. Apply a dab of glue. Push the wire end into the handle and allow to dry (see Fig 2.9).

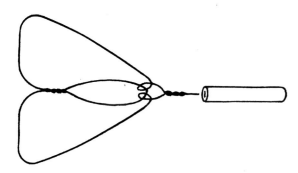

FIG 2.9

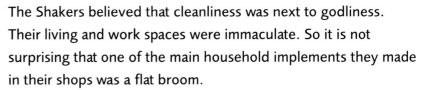

Shaker flat broom

Tools and materials

Raffia (natural)

28-gauge (or finer) craft wire

$^1/_{16}$in (0.1cm) dowel, 2$^1/_2$in (6.3cm) long

Thread (non-metallic gold)

Fine-grade sandpaper

Scissors

Wire cutters

Needle-nose pliers

Craft knife

Sewing needle

Metal straight-edged ruler

Pencil or fine-tipped pen

Bowl with warm water

Paper towels

Finished size

Approximately 3$^1/_2$in (9cm) long

The Shakers believed that cleanliness was next to godliness. Their living and work spaces were immaculate. So it is not surprising that one of the main household implements they made in their shops was a flat broom.

The flat broom was the most modern of Shaker brooms. It had greater sweeping efficiency than its round cousin: the brush fanned out over a wider area. Depending upon the length of the bristle trim, it was used to sweep hardwood or concrete floors.

Broom handles were turned on lathes in the Shaker woodworking shops. The brush of the broom was made from the seed tassel of an annual grass called broomcorn, a tall plant that resembles Indian corn. The broomcorn was bound together, trimmed and then secured to the handle with string.

Because of their quality and the care taken of them, Shaker brooms lasted a long time. To keep the bristles in good condition, they were hung on the wall. In dry climates, owners were encouraged to stand the bristles in a pail of water for 15 minutes every six months to increase the moisture content of the broomcorn. In damp climates, a bleach and water solution prevented mildew from turning the bristles black.

Hang your miniature broom on a hook in your kitchen or stand it in the corner to await an hour of housekeeping.

METHOD

1 Cut approximately 40 pieces of raffia into 4in (10cm) lengths, and soften them in a bowl of warm water. The amount of raffia you need depends upon its thickness and the desired fullness of the broom.

2 For the handle, round off one end of the dowel with fine-grade sandpaper.

3 Once the raffia is softened (about 30 minutes), remove from the water. Squeeze out the excess and blot on paper towels. Before

the raffia dries completely, gather the pieces together. Place the broom handle in the center of the bundle. Wrap the pieces around the bottom third of the broom handle (see Fig 2.10).

4 Cut a length of wire 5–6in (12–15cm) long.

5 Locate the bottom of the broom handle in the bundle. Wrap the wire tightly around the raffia bundle three or four times, $\frac{1}{2}$in (1.25cm) up from the bottom. Secure the end of the wire at the back, by twisting it with the needle-nose pliers. Trim the wire with wire cutters and fold it neatly down.

FIG 2.10

6 Pinch the raffia below the wire to flatten as much as possible and allow it to finish drying. If necessary, place a weight on it.

7 Once dry, use a pencil and a metal ruler to draw two lines on the raffia as a stitching guide. The first line should be below the bottom of the handle. The second should be $\frac{1}{8}$in (0.25cm) below that.

8 Chain stitch across the lines through all the raffia layers making tiny stitches with gold-colored thread. Tie a knot at the last stitch and trim the thread.

9 Using a craft knife, carefully trim the raffia above the wire. Do this by gently rocking the blade from side to side as you turn the handle and push down on the raffia.

10 Reduce the bulk above the wire by gently cutting upward from the wire toward the handle. Be careful not to cut into the handle.

11 Cut across the raffia approximately $\frac{3}{4}$in (2cm) down from the bottom of the lowest line of stitching with scissors.

12 To finish, carefully slice through the lower part of the broom with a craft knife to thin out the raffia straw a little.

Rag rug

Tools and materials

1yd (30cm) cotton fabric cut into $^1/_8$in (0.25cm) strips, or cotton yarn (various colors)

Thread (neutral or contrasting colors)

Foam block, 5 x 6in (12 x 15cm) and $1^1/_2$in (3.8cm) thick

Scissors

Ruler

Pen or pencil

Small-handled paintbrush or smooth stick

Comb

Needle with large eye (to insert a strip of fabric)

80 dressmaker's pins

PVA glue or Fray Check

Finished size

Rag rugs can be made to any length required

'Waste not, want not' goes the old adage. Rather than throw anything away, pioneer women made home furnishings from whatever they had. Rag rugs epitomize this sense of economy: made from old clothes, they were recycled into something new.

Rag rugs were functional first and decorative second. And with the arrival of better-quality carpets, they were relegated to less public areas of the house.

To make a rag rug, fabric was torn into long strips. Tearing produced ragged edges, so the fabric was also cut with scissors, along the lengthwise grain. Other cutting techniques included rolling the fabric and slicing off cookie-shaped pieces. The strips were then sewn together in coordinating colors.

Rag rugs were made from cotton or wool: cotton for areas with heavy wear-and-tear, like the kitchen, and wool for the hallways.

Once the strips were sewn together, they were wound into tight balls about 6in (15cm) in diameter. Inviting friends over to complete this task was a good excuse for parties known as 'lumpa' or rag-sewing bees. These often ended with a square dance.

The 'balls' would then be warped on the loom with a strong, durable thread and fabric strips woven into a variety of functional floor coverings.

Create a miniature rag rug for your country parlor. Wind some rag balls and display them in a basket next to a miniature loom.

METHOD

1 Draw two lines 3in (7.6cm) long and 5in (12cm) apart on the foam block to use as a guide for inserting the pins.

2 Insert 38 pins on each side to form a 'loom'. Alternate their position along the lines (see Fig 2.11). The pins should extend about $^1/_8$in (0.25cm) out of the foam. Next insert pins A, B, C and D.

3 Tie the thread to pin A. Press the pin into the foam to secure. Wrap the thread around pin B. Begin warping the 'loom' by wrapping the thread around the pin closest to B then across to the other side. Weave the thread back and forth between each side (see Fig 2.12). Keep the thread taut. End by wrapping the thread around pin D and securing it to pin C.

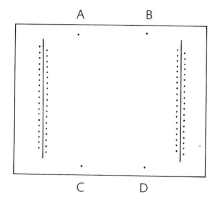

FIG 2.11

4 Once the loom has been warped, use a small paintbrush or smooth stick to create a 'shed'. The 'shed' is the opening created between the layers of thread (warp) as every other thread is pulled up, through which each strip of cloth (weft) is inserted. Weave the shed under and over each thread and slide it down to one end. The shed will be raised on every other 'shot' (or row) to allow for easy insertion of the fabric strip.

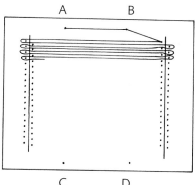

FIG 2.12

5 Thread the needle with thread. Weave five or six rows to start the rug. For every other row, weave the needle under and over the threads. For the alternate row, simply raise the paintbrush up slightly and slide the needle through the opening. 'Beat' (or tidy) the rows into line by pushing back on them lightly with the comb. Be careful not to pull the thread too tightly or your edges will be uneven.

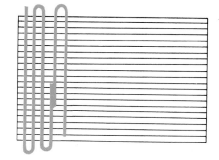

FIG 2.13

6 After the first five or six rows, thread the needle with a fabric strip (weft). Repeat the same technique to the desired length of your rug. When you come to the end of a fabric strip, weave the end neatly into the fiber of the rug. Start a new piece by overlapping it slightly (see Fig 2.13). 'Beat' the rows into line by pushing back on them lightly with the comb.

7 Finish the rug by weaving another five or six rows of thread. Be careful not to pull the thread too tightly. 'Beat' the thread into place with a comb.

8 Before cutting the rug from the loom, apply a line of diluted white glue or Fray Check to the woven thread ends; this will stop the rug from unraveling. Carefully cut across the threads 1/4in (0.5cm) from the ends to make a fringe.

Checkerboard and checkers

Tools and materials

3/32in (0.2cm) piece of
*   basswood*
Polymer clay (eg. Fimo) (red
*   and black)*
Acrylic paint (off-white and red)
Fine-grade sandpaper
Craft knife
Metal straight-edged ruler
Paintbrush
Razor blade
Fine-tipped permanent marker
*   (black)*
Square
Pencil
Ceramic tile or sheets of
*   aluminum foil*
PVA glue

Finished size

1 3/8in (3.5cm) square

Checkers originated around 200 BC in Egypt. Played by aristocrats, the game was adopted by the Greeks and the Romans and, after many years of traveling east, the game reached the Chinese, too. In England, it was known as draughts.

The American version of the game features two sets of 12 disks. Normally, one set is red, the other white. Each player has a set of disks. The game board consists of an eight-inch square grid, containing 64 green and tan squares. Noncompetition sets feature red and black disks on a red and black board.

The basis of the game of checkers is to capture all of your opponent's disks while ensuring that your own reach the other side of the board. To begin, each player places their set of 12 disks on the first row of coloured squares. Players can make only one move per turn. If a player is unable to move, he or she loses the game. Each disk can move only one square diagonally or one square forward and the square must already be vacant.

To make progress across the board, the player must jump their disk over their opponent's. Players can make a multiple jump, using one disk only, if there are empty squares between those containing the opponent's disk. When a disk reaches the last row, a second checker is placed on top and is called a king. Kings operate the same as regular checkers except they can also move backward into spaces.

Famous checker players include Napoleon, General Ulysses S. Grant, Edgar Allen Poe and Andrew Carnegie.

Add a miniature game of checkers to a children's playroom scene. Recreate the feel of a Norman Rockwell painting by placing the checkerboard and checkers on a miniature picnic table in a park setting.

METHOD

1 Cut the wood into a 1³⁄₈in (3.5cm) square. Sand smooth the edges with a piece of fine-grade sandpaper.

2 Paint both sides of the square with off-white acrylic paint. Put to one side to dry. Sand the surface smooth with the sandpaper. Apply a second coat and again, leave to dry.

3 Draw a frame around the outside edge of the wood, ³⁄₁₆in (0.4cm) in from the edge. With a pencil, make marks every ⅛in (0.25cm) along this frame until you have a total of eight marks on each side. Draw along the marks with a pencil to form a grid.

4 Score along each line using the metal ruler and craft knife. Press down gently to form a small indentation.

5 Paint the grid with red acrylic paint. Be careful not to paint outside the outer frame. Allow to dry.

6 Carefully fill in every other square with the black marker, starting in the top right-hand corner. Fill in the squares, moving across and down. This forms the checkerboard pattern.

7 Roll the red polymer clay into a snake-like roll, ³⁄₃₂in (0.2cm) in diameter. Do the same with the black polymer clay. Bake according to the manufacturer's instructions. Allow to cool.

8 Slice the roll into checkers, ¹⁄₁₆in (0.1cm) thick, using a single-edged razor blade. You will need 12 checkers of each color.

9 Glue the checkers to the checkerboard (see Fig 2.14). At the start of the game, each side should have three rows of checkers on only the black squares.

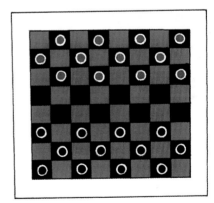

FIG 2.14

Mailbox

Tools and materials

Sheet of smooth card

Acrylic paint (traditional silver, black, or own colors)

$^1/_{16}$in (0.1cm) piece of basswood

Sandpaper

Paintbrushes

Metal straight-edged ruler

Sharp scissors

Pencil

Dressmaker's pin

Wire cutter

Needle-nose pliers

Craft knife

Jigsaw or other small saw

Large needle

Small block of softwood or piece of heavy card

Tacky glue

Finished size

1$^1/_8$in (3cm) high by $^7/_8$in (2.2cm) wide

The history of delivering mail can be traced to Roman times, when a communication was delivered by messenger on horseback. A *positus* or 'post', was a stopping place for messengers to switch horses before continuing on.

Much later, in America, stagecoaches carried the mail between towns. Inadequate roads, difficult terrain and thieves meant it took up to three weeks to deliver a letter. Things got a little faster with the Pony Express. Riders on horseback carried messages coast to coast via a 2,000-mile trail which took eight days. It was eventually replaced by the telegraph.

In 1902, the United States Postal Service instituted a service that continues today: free rural delivery. Patrons often customized the receptacles for their mail, but many provided inadequate shelter. In 1915, the Post Office commissioned a design by Roy Jorelman, a postal employee, for a standard rural mailbox. The flag on the side was raised to signal that there was mail to be posted. When the mailman picked it up, the flag was placed downward.

Today's mailboxes often reflect the owner's sense of style. You will find many whimsical colours and designs. In rural areas, you'll occasionally see one painted white with black spots. Chances are the owner is a dairy farmer.

Make a few miniature mailboxes, using the traditional aluminum finish, or design your own. Why not mount it to a post or porch rail for authenticity?

METHOD

1 Cut a strip of card, 1$^1/_2$ x 2$^1/_2$in (3.8 x 6.3cm) in size, for the 'roof', and another strip, 1 x 1$^1/_2$in (2.5 x 3.8cm) in size, for the base.

2 On the vertical sides of the base strip, mark a line $^1/_{16}$in (0.1cm) in from both sides with a pencil (see Fig 2.15). With a craft knife, score along the pencil mark, but without cutting through. Fold up both edges to a 90° angle. This forms the base (see Fig 2.16).

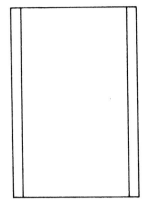

3 Apply a thin line of glue along the inside of one folded edge. Attach one long side of the 'roof' part and allow to dry. Take the other long side of the 'roof' and attach to the inner edge of the other side of the base (see Fig 2.17). This forms the basic mailbox.

4 Now for the arch-shaped back end. Take another small piece of card. Position the mailbox on one end onto the piece of card and, using the metal-edged ruler to keep it in place, trace around the end of the mailbox with the pencil. Make a small X on the card to mark the side of the card that will be glued inside. Your tracing should flare out slightly at the base where the sides will be glued. Cut out the piece following the traced line. Glue the piece to the back end of the mailbox (the end used for tracing), with the X facing inward. Allow to dry.

5 Now for the door end. Draw another line on the remaining card with a pencil. Follow the method for step 4, tracing around the upturned mailbox as before. Again, make a small X on the card to mark the side that will be glued. Draw a line $\frac{1}{4}$in (0.5cm) down from the base. Make a mark at the center of the line. From the center, draw two lines: one to each corner of the base to form a triangle. Erase the base line (the dashed line in Fig 2.18A). Cut out the piece following the traced line and the triangle.

6 Cut a strip of card, $\frac{3}{8}$ x $2\frac{3}{8}$in (0.25 x 6cm) in size. Glue the strip to the edge of the traced piece starting just above the base (where it flares out slightly). The strip should stand up from the traced piece (see Fig 2.18B). This forms the rim of the mailbox door.

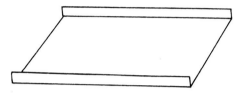

FIG 2.15

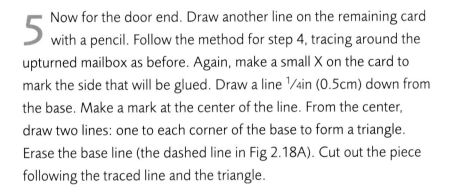

FIG 2.16

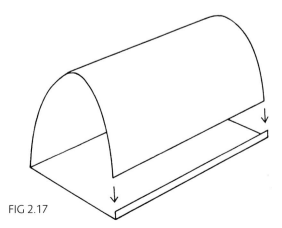

FIG 2.17

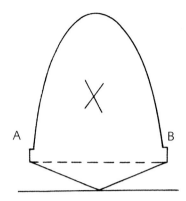

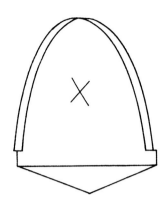

FIG 2.18A   FIG 2.18B

7 Dry-fit the door piece over the end of the mailbox for proper alignment. Turn the mailbox so that the bottom end faces up. Draw a line on the mailbox cover where it meets the bottom. Remove the door and score along the line with a craft knife. Bend the cover at the scored line to form a hinge.

8 Place the back of the door on the open end. Glue the triangle part onto the outside bottom of the base. Close the door.

9 Place the mailbox on the piece of basswood or a piece of sturdy cardboard. Trace around the outline. Cut out around the tracing. Glue the wood to the bottom of the mailbox.

10 Paint the mailbox inside and out. (Do not add water to dilute the paint.) Allow the mailbox to dry thoroughly before continuing. Close the door again to make sure the paper has not warped with the paint.

FIG 2.19

11 Now for the flag post. Cut a pin to a length of 1in (2.5cm) using a wire cutter. Sand the cut end to remove any sharp edges. Bend the pin ¼in (0.5cm) up from the head into a U using the needle-nose pliers (see Fig 2.19).

12 Place a small block of softwood on the inside of the mailbox. With the opening of the mailbox facing you, hold the wood steady to cushion the pinhole. With a long needle, poke a hole through this side, approximately ¼in (0.5cm) in from the opening, just above the base. Remove the block. From the inside, insert the pin through the hole up to the pinhead for a flag post.

13 Cut a strip of card ¼ x ½in (0.5 x 1.25cm) long. Fold the strip in half lengthwise to form a square. Apply glue to the inside of the square. Wrap the square around the flag post at the top. Pinch the sides together to secure it firmly to the post. Paint the flag with red acrylic paint.

14 Cut a strip of card, ⅛ x ½in (0.25 x 1.6cm) in size. Wrap one end around the base of the needle to form a curl. This forms a spring to keep the door closed. Place the curl on top of the door. Glue the other end to the top of the mailbox.

15 Cut a strip of card ⅛ x ¼in (0.25 x 0.5cm) in size. Wrap one end around the base of the needle to form a curl. This forms the handle to open the mailbox. Glue the base of the handle with the curl facing out onto the door just below the spring.

16 Paint the spring and handle to match the rest of the mailbox. You may wish to paint your miniature family's name or house number on the side for authenticity (see Fig 2.20).

FIG 2.20

Shoo-fly quilt

Tools and materials

18-count cross-stitch fabric (or
* 22-count, 32-count, etc.)*
Embroidery floss, 1¹/₂ skeins
* (dark blue)*
Fusible webbing
Backing material (ivory felt)
Scissors
Needle
Embroidery hoop
Iron

Finished size

3⁵/₈ x 5in (9.3 x 12cm)

Quilting was first introduced to Europe during the Crusades, when soldiers brought back warm, padded clothing made from fabric composed of three stitched layers. The craft of quilting spread across the continent and was eventually brought to America by immigrants.

Quilting was a practical craft, to help keep out the cold, but it also became an outlet for creativity. Quilting bees were an opportunity to renew friendships and swap news.

As garments wore out, women saved the scraps for their next project. These remnants were used to patch older quilts, and as the basis for 'crazy quilts'. Eventually, the remnants were cut into same-sized triangles and hexagons and arranged to form a pattern.

Over the years, the geometric designs became more elaborate. Many patterns were named after everyday items such as fruit, insects, famous people and even food: for example, the shoo-fly quilt.

'Shoo fly' most likely originated from the lyrics of a Civil War song: 'shoo fly, don't bother me'. Shoo fly also refers to a shuffling dance, or an open pie filled with molasses and brown sugar. The pie was so sweet that it attracted flies and housewives would have to literally 'shoo' the flies away.

The shoo-fly pattern forms a nine-patch quilt, the most popular style after the four-patch quilt. It is a simple block repeat that can be adjusted to fit any size quilt from a pillow to a king-size bed.

When the shoo-fly pattern is completed in green and yellow on white, it is called 'Chinese coin'. A change in color in an original pattern frequently gave the pattern a new name.

METHOD

1 Work the cross-stitch pattern using two strands of floss. Stitch only the dark squares, for a quilted look. Follow the color guide shown (see Fig 2.21) as reference.

2 Remove fabric from the embroidery hoop. If soiled at all, wash in cold water and iron dry. Clip any hanging threads from the back.

3 Cut fabric to within $\frac{1}{2}$in (1cm) on all sides. Fold under $\frac{1}{4}$in (0.5cm). Miter the corners to reduce bulk. Iron flat.

4 If making the quilt as a wall hanging, use ivory felt as a backing material, with fusible webbing. Cut both the same size as the quilt. Apply the webbing to the felt following manufacturer's instructions. For a bed quilt, use a thinner material to back your quilt.

5 Apply the fused side of the webbed backing to the wrong side of the top, again consulting manufacturer's instructions.

FIG 2.21

Western

Belt ⭐ Bedroll

Bolo tie ⭐ Canteen

Calf-roping lariat ⭐ Branding iron

Chaparreras ⭐ Cowboy boots

Cowboy hat

Cowboy herding horses, 1887

T o 'go west' was a reflection of the pursuit of the 'American Dream'. Unlike the pilgrims who came to the United States to avoid religious persecution and gain economic freedom, settlers who traveled westward wanted to escape the crowded cities, and yearned for the chance to strike it rich in the California gold rush.

The cowboys of the old West who had experienced the devastating effects of the American Civil War (1861–5) shared some of these motivations. Many Confederate soldiers saw driving cattle as a way of making their fortunes and having the freedom to be their own boss. Cowboys had to be self-reliant, courageous and tough – the same qualities that helped them survive the horrors of war.

The heyday of the cowboy spanned the period from 1866 until open-range ranching ended with the introduction of barbed wire in 1887. During this time, cowboys drove cattle from southern – primarily Texan – ranches to the nearest railroad town, often hundreds of miles away. From there, the cattle were shipped east.

The cowboys followed specific routes called trails: the Chisholm, Santa Fe, California and Goodnight-Loving trails are famous examples. They wove through the plains and mountains *en route* to the big stockyards, the most well-known of which was Abilene, Kansas.

Television and movies romanticize the life of the cowboy. During the 1950s and 1960s, families avidly followed the adventures of heroic screen cowboys Roy Rogers, Hopalong Cassidy and the Lone Ranger.

The Lone Ranger was a heroic screen cowboy in the 1950s and his popularity endures today

The reality of a cowboy's life was anything but glamorous. The work was hard, fraught with danger and the pay poor. A herd of cattle might bring a rancher $100,000, but the cowboy earned only $200 for six months' work.

Women traveled west, too. Tired of the constraints of Victorian life, women looked to the West for escape. Real and fictional cowgirls like Martha 'Calamity Jane' Cannary and Phoebe 'Annie Oakley' Moses showed an independent character and a bold spirit. They needed to be made of sturdy stock to negotiate the hardships.

Some believed that a woman's place was in the home, and many who favored independence were treated with prejudice. Frontier women were often considered prostitutes and, in extreme cases, murdered.

Women who wanted to 'go west' had few options: the most common was to find work as schoolteachers, so some masqueraded as men. They joined cattle drives, roped steers, broke broncos, at times better than their male peers. Often, their real gender was only discovered after their death.

Other women traveled with their husbands, who hoped to make their fortunes in cattle or live on the open plains. They had to adapt to a life of manual labor and loneliness. Despite these things, the majority rose to the challenge, enjoying the relative freedom of open spaces.

Annie Oakley entertains with feats of skillful marksmanship, as featured in the Police Gazette, *1892*

Belt

Tools and materials

Thin leather (black)

3 miniature conchos (jewelry findings: bead caps)

A jewelry finding (for the buckle)

Scissors

Metal straight-edged ruler

Needle-nose pliers

Needle

PVA glue

Staple

Finished size

With a buckle: 3¹/₈in (8cm) long

The cowboy's tight pants did not really require a belt, but in the early days of the old West, he needed one to hold his holster and gun. A wide belt was also used to help ease the strain of working with horses and cattle by supporting the back and protecting his internal organs.

Later, the belt became more decorative than functional. It was made of calfskin or horsehide and carved with natural motifs. Leather carving was a skill the cowboy inherited from the Mexicans, who in turn adapted it from the Spanish.

The belt became an excuse for showing off elaborate silver buckles: the cowboy's metal of choice. The West was home to silver mines and the metal was widely used by the Mexicans and Native Americans to decorate their clothes and animals.

Use this miniature belt to accent a pair of jeans or chaps.

METHOD

1 With a craft knife, cut a thin strip of black leather 3¹/₈ x ¹/₈in (8 x 0.25cm) in size.

2 Cut off the corners from one end of the strip of leather to form a neat V shape.

3 Punch three equidistant holes leading up to the V-shaped end with a needle (see Fig 3.1).

FIG 3.1

4 Fold the leather strip back ¹/₈in (0.25cm) on the opposite end. Punch a hole in the center of the fold. Clip a staple in half. Insert the shortest end through the hole (see Fig 3.2). Glue the fold down.

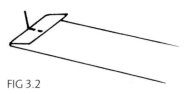

5 Bend the jewelry finding with a pair of needle-nose pliers to form a U. Glue the finding to the folded edge of the leather strip to form the buckle.

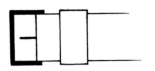

FIG 3.2

6 Cut another strip of leather ³⁄₈ x ¹⁄₄in (1 x 0.5cm) long to form a loop. Wrap this piece around the belt near the buckle (see Fig 3.3). Glue the loop ends to the back of the belt.

7 Evenly space the decorative jewelry findings onto the front of the belt, then glue them into place.

FIG 3.3

Bedroll

In the days of the old West, the cowboy was often forced to sleep under the stars.

After a hard day, he would dismount his horse, start a fire and then get a little sleep. The cowboy's bed was unrolled at night and rolled up again the next morning, hence its name. It was lined with blankets, quilts or clothes to keep him warm, and once rolled, also carried his money and a few personal possessions. It was his home away from home.

If traveling in a group, bedrolls were carried on a dedicated wagon. If alone, it was tied to his saddle with a leather thong along with his cooking utensils.

Lean a miniature bedroll up against a tree or wagon to complement a Western scene.

Tools and materials
Worn piece of 2 x 6in (5 x 15cm)
  fabric (eg. old flannel shirt)
Small, thin piece of leather
2 jump rings (jewelry findings)
Scissors
Metal straight-edged ruler
PVA glue

Finished size
2in (5cm) long

METHOD

1 Cut a strip of fabric 2 x 6in (5 x 15cm) long, or longer if the fabric is thinner.

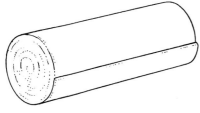

FIG 3.4

2 Roll the material up lengthwise into a tight roll. Secure with a dab of glue (see Fig 3.4).

3 For the leather straps, cut two leather strips $^{1}/_{8}$ x $2^{3}/_{4}$in (0.25 x 7cm) long. Cut an additional two strips $^{1}/_{8}$ x $^{1}/_{2}$in (0.25 x 1cm) in size.

FIG 3.5

4 Clip corners at one end of each of the $2^{3}/_{4}$in (7cm) lengths of leather to form a neat V shape (see Fig 3.5).

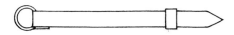

FIG 3.6

5 At the opposite ends, slip on a jump ring. Fold the end of the leather strips under, about $^{1}/_{4}$in (0.5cm), to hold the ring in position (see Fig 3.6). Glue down.

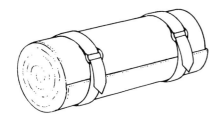

FIG 3.7

6 Wrap the leather strips around the bedroll approximately $^{3}/_{8}$in (1cm) in from each end. Place the V through the ring and pull firmly to form a loop.

7 To check that the rings are level, align each one so it is on the same side of the bedroll. Make a small mark $^{1}/_{2}$in (1.25cm) in from where the tip of the V falls on both strips (see Fig 3.7). Once measured, remove the strips from the bedroll.

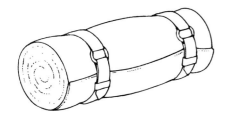

FIG 3.8

8 Wrap the smaller strips of leather around the longer ones at the mark made in step 7 to form a strap loop (see Fig 3.8). Apply a dab of glue in the back to secure.

9 Wrap the longer strips around the roll again, taking the V through the ring, around the bedroll and through the loop. Secure the V with a dab of glue. The rings, V shapes and loops should all line up correctly (see Fig 3.9).

FIG 3.9

Bolo tie

Everything in a cowboy's life reflected his work, including his clothes and accessories. The bolo tie was named after a 'boleadora', a leather device used by Argentine gauchos to bring down a running animal. Boleadoras are three rawhide thongs joined at one end. The other ends are tipped with metal or wooden balls or leather-covered stones. While the gaucho would use the full-size boleadora like a lariat, cowboys wore a miniature version of this tool around their neck *in lieu* of a regular tie, usually to dress up a Western-style shirt.

Most bolo ties are made from braided leather accented with silver tips. An adjustable jeweled slide secures the tie. While this may hint at fashion, the leather and silver represent strength and durability, both highly prized qualities for the cowboy.

Dress your cowboy in a bolo tie and he will be ready to squire the ladies to the dance hall.

Tools and materials

Metal snap or post earring back
Waxed linen cord or thin leather
  cord, 4in (10cm) in length
2 silver French hook ear wires
  (or other metal tip source)
Small piece of turquoise or bead
Scissors
Wire cutter
Needle-nose pliers
PVA glue

METHOD

1 Cut one strip of waxed linen cord or thin leather cord 4in (10cm) long.

2 Feed each end of the cord through the earring back or the holes in the snap back to create the slide. If using a snap back, you may need to clip off the bump of the snap. If you are using the earring back, gently squeeze the back with needle-nose pliers to close the rings around the cord.

3 Clip off the loop end from the French hook ear wires and remove the bead stopper. Carefully thread the bead stopper onto the ends of the cord to create the bolo tips. Apply a dab of glue on the ends. Twist the bead stopper into the cord to help secure the tip.

4 Glue the bead or stone to the flat side of the slide to complete the tie.

Finished size
2in (5cm) in length

Canteen

Tools and materials

Thin leather, suede or canvas

A miniature concho (jewelry findings: bead cap)

A seed bead

2 turned wooden plates, ³⁄₄in (2cm) in diameter

Acrylic paint (black) (optional)

Scissors

Metal straight-edged ruler

PVA glue

We can go days without food, but not water. This posed a problem for cowboys driving cattle through patches of dry country. An insufficient water supply meant certain death.

Wherever there was water, a cowboy stopped, drank his fill and then replenished his supply to carry him to the next water source. The water was kept in a metal container called a canteen or in a waterproof canvas bag. Most had stoppers for easy access and straps so that the water could be slung over a shoulder or the side of a saddle.

Hang your miniature canteen from your cowboy's saddle.

METHOD

1 Glue the two plates together to form the body of the canteen.

2 Cut two 1in (2.5cm) circles from the leather or canvas. Cut two strips of leather or canvas ¹⁄₄in (0.5cm) wide. One strip should be 1¹⁄₄in (3.2cm) long, and the other should be 5in (12cm) long.

3 Glue the leather circles around each side of the canteen, and trim as necessary.

4 Select which part will be the top of the canteen. Glue the shortest strip over the seam in the center.

5 Glue the concho (metal jewelry finding) in the top center of the canteen. Glue the seed bead on top of the concho to form the cap. Dab a little black acrylic paint on the cap to take off the shine.

6 Fold the 5in (12cm) strip in half to locate the center. Glue the center of the strip to the bottom of the canteen. Glue the long strip over the seam to meet the short strip. Clip the ends to form a V. Overlap the ends slightly to form a shoulder strap. Glue into place.

Finished size

2³⁄₈in (6cm) long with the strap and ³⁄₄in (2cm) in diameter

Calf-roping lariat

The lariat or lasso was one of the cowboy's essential tools. When the calves were old enough, the ranch hands – many of whom were former cowboys – would gather together to cull the calves from their mothers in preparation for branding.

The cowboys would throw the lariat's noose around the calf's neck and pull on it, causing the calf to stumble and fall. When the calf was down, the cowboy would use the lariat to tie the calf's legs together. Once bound, it was branded, earmarked and if male, castrated, and finally released to join its mother.

Lassoing an animal in action took hours of practice. The best cowboys could achieve it in less than a minute without harming the animal. Competitions to find the fastest roper in the West were one form of recreation during slow periods. These rodeos often held calf-roping events, with a silver buckle as first prize.

Hang this miniature lariat over a fence post, hay bale or barn door for an authentic scene.

Tools and materials

Waxed linen cord, natural color, 35in (88cm) in length
Thread (brown or gold)
Scissors
PVA glue

Finished size

1¹/₂in (3.8cm) long, but length can vary

METHOD

1 Cut the cord to a length of 35in (88cm) long. Fold down ¹/₂in 1.25cm) to form a loop or noose.

2 Wrap the thread around the base of the loop to secure it to the cord (see Fig 3.10). Apply a dab of glue.

3 Insert the opposite end of the cord through the loop. Pull it through. Hold your thumb and forefinger about 1¹/₂in (3.8cm) apart. Lay the loop on the top of your fingers. Wrap the cord around your fingers several times to form the curled lariat. Leave about 1in (2.5cm) of cord at the end.

4 Wrap the remaining 1in (2.5cm) around the cord a few times. Press to hold in place.

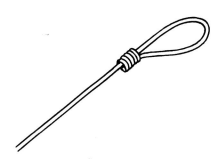

FIG 3.10

Branding iron

Tools and materials

Card

Large paperclip

Fine-grade sandpaper

Acrylic paint (matte black)

Scissors

Metal straight-edged ruler

Wire cutter

Needle-nose pliers

Paintbrush

Craft knife

PVA glue

Finished size

3¹/₈in (8cm) long

Branding has an ignominious history. Spanish conquistador and explorer, Hernando Cortez, introduced it to North America when he burned a C on the cheeks of his Native American slaves.

Before driving his herds of cattle to market, a rancher needed to ensure his stock was protected against thievery, and to identify them if they strayed. To do this, he branded the calves with a hot iron.

Branding took place once cowboys separated the calves from the cows. Calves were wrestled to the ground and bound at the feet. A red-hot branding iron was then applied to the animal's hide and, by way of a further precautionary measure, its ear was slit. To differentiate between similar brands, some ranchers applied it to the animal's neck, others to the shoulder.

The brand was the owner's mark. Ranchers would design their own proprietary brand with letters, figures, pictures or other motifs. The 'two hearts' brand featured two intertwined hearts, while the 'mashed O' brand resembled an oval. A cowboy sometimes branded an animal with a heart as a way of declaring his love to someone. The Christian cross, anchor and swastika were the most common picture brands. The swastika represented the sun and creation, although it took on a very different symbolism during World War II when the Nazis adopted it as the symbol of the Third Reich.

Brands were registered with the county clerk. If a rancher did not register his brand, the government could potentially confiscate his animals.

This miniature Circle W is easy to create. Use it as a decorative accent in a country home or place it near a campfire in preparation for branding.

METHOD

1 Straighten the paperclip with the pliers. Roughen the surface with sandpaper to encourage the paint to adhere.

2 Cut the extended paperclip to a length of $3\frac{1}{8}$in (8.2cm). Create a loop on one end with the pliers.

3 Paint the paperclip with matte black paint. Set aside to dry.

4 Cut a strip of card $\frac{3}{32}$ x $1\frac{1}{8}$in (0.2 x 3cm). Wrap the strip around a thick pencil, overlapping the ends slightly. Secure the strip with a dab of glue. This should create a circle approximately $\frac{5}{16}$in (0.8cm) in diameter.

5 Cut another strip of card to the same size. Bend the strip into a W. You may want to score the card with the back of the craft knife before folding it. To do this, run the craft knife blade lightly across the card, just enough to break the surface, but not enough to cut through. Score or bend the center of the strip. Score or bend the strip again $\frac{1}{4}$in (0.5cm) at either side of the center.

6 Test-fit the W by placing it in the center of the circle. Apply a dab of glue at each point of the W that touches the circle. Place the W inside the circle (see Fig 3.11). Adjust if necessary with the remaining portion of the paperclip. Allow the glue to dry thoroughly. Paint the brand with matte black paint.

7 Place the brand on a flat surface after the paint has dried. Apply a dab of glue to the inside center of the W. Insert the paperclip handle. Touch up with further paint, if necessary.

FIG 3.11

Chaparreras

Tools and materials

Piece of thin leather or suede

Jump ring (jewelry finding)
  (gold or silver)

Card

Matching thread

Quilting thread or other heavy
  thread (for lacing)

Scissors

Needle

Sewing machine (optional)

PVA glue

Finished size

3¹/₈in (8cm) long

Chaparreras or 'chaps' are a waist-to-ankle apron, usually made of leather or animal skins. They are divided up the middle and tied with leather straps at the waist and knees. Like an apron, they have no back portion or seat.

'Chaparreras' means 'leg armor' in Spanish. And a pair of chaps did just that: they protected the cowboy from saddle sores, from ripping his clothes on sharp objects and, importantly, kept him warm in cold climates.

The style of chaps varied with location. In the North, they were made of two separate leather 'barrels' held together by a belt. Worn plain, without a fringe along the length of each leg, they were called 'closed leg' chaps. They were worn to deflect snow and keep the rider warm. With a fringe, they were called 'shotgun' chaps.

'Batwing' chaps kept the Southern cowboy from losing his skin when his horse took a shortcut through a mesquite patch. The open design of the batwing chaps helped keep him cool.

In the blizzard country of Montana, the Dakotas and Wyoming, cowboys wore 'wooly' chaps made of angora goatskin, sheepskin and even bearskin.

Make many pairs in different styles to hang in a miniature barn.

METHOD

1 Copying the templates, cut the chaps out of leather or suede (see Fig 3.12). You will need two of the leg of the chaps.

2 With right sides together, stitch along the side seams of both legs (see Fig 3.13). With your fingers, press the seams open and clip them. Turn the legs right side out.

3 With the longest side of the chaps facing down, slightly overlap the front of the two legs (see Fig 3.14). Secure the connection with a dab of glue.

4 Fold over ¼in (0.5cm) of one end of the belt. Insert the jump ring into the fold. Glue in place.

5 Glue the short strip to the other end of the belt, overlapping about ¼in (0.5cm) (see Fig 3.15).

6 Glue the belt to the front side of the chaps. Center the point of the belt at the crotch.

7 Close up the opening with quilting thread in a crisscross motion (see Fig 3.16).

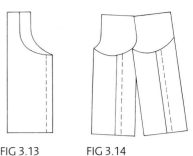

FIG 3.13   FIG 3.14

FIG 3.15

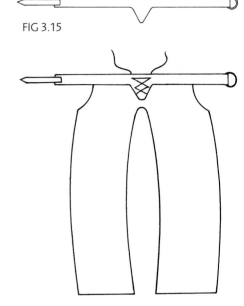

FIG 3.16

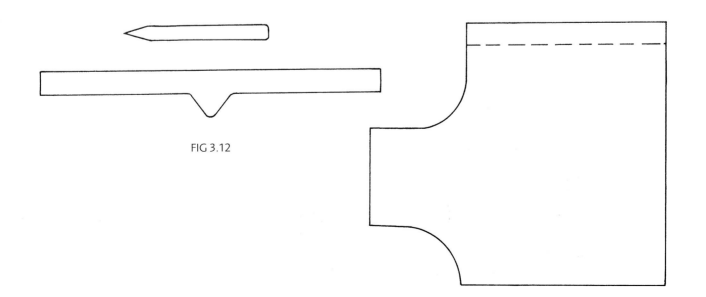

FIG 3.12

Cowboy hat

Tools and materials

Thin suede

Waxed linen cord or thin leather cord (for the hatband)

Scrap of polymer clay (for hat form) (eg. Sculpey)

Small square of aluminum foil

Scissors

Rubber band

Round toothpick

Small plastic bowl

Craft knife

Ceramic tile or sheets of aluminum foil

PVA glue

Water

Finished size

1¹/₂in (3.8cm) in diameter and ¹/₂in (1.25cm) high

Movie stars, kings, US presidents and outlaws have worn the cowboy hat. For real cowboys it served to protect against the elements. The high crown kept the cowboy cool and the wide brim prevented exposure to the sun, driving rain, wind and dust.

The most famous cowboy hat is the Stetson. Invented by hat maker John B. Stetson, it was made from felt and known as 'The Boss of the Plains'. A classic Stetson has a 5in (12cm) brim, a high crown and a 'pencil-rolled' edge.

While the Stetson has been glorified in movies and TV – movie star Tom Mix wore his at every personal appearance – in reality, cowboys wore any kind of hat, as long as it was efficient.

The cowboy hat was multi-functional. It became a bucket for scooping water, though it was never capable of holding ten gallons. It was placed under the head as a pillow. It was also utilized as a fan to encourage the first sparks of a campfire, and it acted as a signaling device for fellow travelers.

Cowboy hats came in three colors: brown, gray and black felt. In the movies, good guys wore white hats and villains wore black, but real cowboys wore whatever was available.

Felt was the fabric of choice for cowboys because it was easy to shape. The brim's width, the peak's height and the way a cowboy creased his hat let others know where he was from. Northern cowboys wore a hat with a narrow brim and low crown while those from the South needed the shade provided by a wide brim and higher crown.

Hats were decorated with hatbands, which were more than an esthetic accent. They gave the cowboy a sense of individuality. Some hatbands were made out of horsehair, rattlesnake hide or leather studded with silver. Others were made from beads, braided gold or silver wires.

Whether your miniature cowboy hat is added to a Western scene or general store or placed in a contemporary setting, it comes with an authentic Western attitude.

METHOD

1 Make the hat form. Roll some polymer clay into a $1\frac{1}{2}$in (3.8cm) long sausage, $\frac{3}{4}$in (2cm) in diameter. Slightly round over one end. Roll the end between your thumb and forefinger to make an oval. Hold that end between your thumb and forefinger. Create an indentation with a toothpick. The indentation should be about $\frac{1}{8}$in (0.25cm) deep and shaped like a V.

2 Bake the form according to manufacturer's directions. Allow to cool thoroughly.

3 For the hat itself, place a piece of foil over the hat form. Smooth the foil into the indentation and around the top of the form.

4 Cut one suede circle 2in (5cm) in diameter. Cut two suede circles $1\frac{1}{2}$in (3.8cm) in diameter.

5 Mix approximately 1tsp of PVA glue with $\frac{1}{2}$tsp water in a small bowl. Soak the 2in (5cm) diameter circle in the mixture. Work the mixture into the suede with your fingers and squeeze out the excess. Place the leather onto the foil-covered hat form. Pull the leather down tightly over the form. Secure the leather at the base with a rubber band. Work the leather down into the indentation with a toothpick. Set aside. Allow the leather to dry overnight.

6 Place one of the $1\frac{1}{2}$in (3.8cm) circles into the glue and water mixture. Work the mixture into the suede with your fingers and squeeze out the excess. Place the circle on a piece of foil. Allow to dry overnight.

7 Once the leather is thoroughly dry, remove the hat crown from the hat form. Clip the leather around the crown from the outside edge to the base of the rubber band line. Gently fold up the clipped edges.

8 Draw a ³/₄in (2cm) circle in the center of the 1¹/₂in (3.8cm) glued circle for the brim. Carefully cut out this inner circle with a craft knife and discard. The remaining donut-shaped circle is the brim. Slide the brim over the top of the hat crown. Glue the crown's clipped edges to the bottom of the brim.

9 Again, draw a ³/₄in (2cm) circle in the center of the remaining 1¹/₂in (3.8cm) circle. Carefully cut out this circle with a craft knife and discard. Dab a little glue around the underside of the brim. Glue the remaining donut-shaped circle to the underside of the brim.

10 Dab a little more glue around the base of the crown where it meets the brim. Glue the cord around the crown base to form a hat band, slightly overlapping the edges.

Cowboy boots

Tools and materials

Thin leather

Sheet of craft foam (brown or black)

Cotton wool ball

Card

Scissors

Fine-tipped permanent marker (to match leather, plus one contrasting color)

Metal straight-edged ruler

Craft knife

Pencil

Toothpick

PVA glue

Nancy Sinatra, daughter of the famous crooner, Frank, had one hit record entitled 'These Boots Are Made for Walking'. Those who have worn them know that Nancy definitely was not singing about a pair of cowboy boots. They were practical as long as the cowboy stayed on his horse, but walking long distances across uneven ground on a 2in heel was very uncomfortable.

The cowboy boot was adapted from Spanish riding boots which the Conquistadores brought to Mexico. The design was elegant and the shape practical. The sharp toe helped the cowboy catch the stirrup and the elevated heel prevented his foot from sliding through the stirrup.

The boot's high cut helped the cowboy avoid cuts and scrapes from mesquite brush. Worn over the pants, they kept the stirrup leathers from rubbing against his legs preventing bruised ankles and chafing. Because most boots were knee-high, they also kept out grit and dirt.

Early cowboy boots were made from horsehide or mule skin. Later versions were made of leather and came with elaborate stitching, which kept the boot's lining and exterior leather together better than any glue or adhesive, and also helped to stiffen the boot.

Today's cowboy 'wannabe' prefers boots made from materials such as snake skin, ostrich or kangaroo hide. Custom-made boots sport decorative cut-outs. For those with cash to burn, boot makers will add silver, gold or precious gems to the design, turning what was once a functional item into a status symbol.

These miniature cowboy boots would look great in a Western scene. For a naughty touch, have them peeping out from under a bed in a miniature brothel.

Finished size
Each boot is 1¹⁄₄ x ⁷⁄₈in
(3.2 x 2.2cm) in size

METHOD

1 Transfer the boot patterns onto card (see Fig 3.17). For each boot, you will need to cut the number of pieces of each template listed in the panel, right.

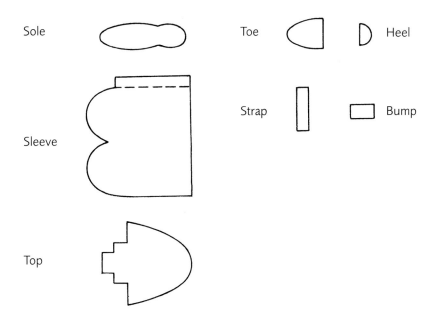

Sole

Toe

Heel

Sleeve

Strap

Bump

Top

FIG 3.17

	LEATHER	FOAM
Sole	4	
Sleeve	2	
Top	2	
Heel	2	2
Toe		2
Bump		2
Strap	4	

FIG 3.18

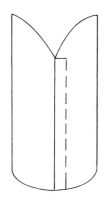

FIG 3.19

2 With wrong sides facing, glue two soles together.

3 Next, glue the bump onto the center of one side of the heel (see Fig 3.18).

4 Overlap the back seam over the tab of the sleeve using a pencil as a jig (see Fig 3.19 for back view, showing the seam). Make sure a V is formed at the top of the seam. Glue into place.

5 Place a dab of glue around the bottom of the sleeve. Glue the sleeve to the top of the sole. Use the bump as a stop to prevent gluing the sides of the sleeve together. Pinch the sides to form an elongated oval.

6 Place the top with the right side facing down on a flat surface. Lay the toe approximately ⅛in (0.25cm) back from the tip of the toe, in the center (see Fig 3.20). Do not glue the pieces together.

7 Fold back the very tip of the top. Glue it to the tip of the toe (see Fig 3.21).

8 Make a small slit on each side of the toe with a craft knife (see Fig 3.22). Glue the sides onto the toe.

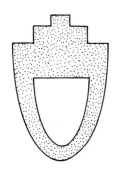

FIG 3.20

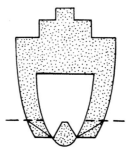

FIG 3.21

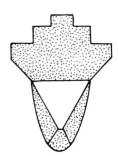

FIG 3.22

9 Turn the piece so that the toe is on a flat surface. Stuff the toe with a bit of cotton wool using the tip of a toothpick. Do not fill past the edge of the foam toe. Shape the toe with your fingers. If it is too tight, remove some of the cotton wool.

10 Glue the toe to the top of the sole so the edge of the foam toe meets the boot sleeve. Pull the stepped portion of the top up and glue it to the boot sleeve. The sides should stick out like wings. Glue the wings around the boot sleeve just above the sole.

11 Glue the wrong side of the leather heel to the foam heel. Glue the foam side of the heel to the bottom of the sole.

12 Pinch a boot strap in half between your fingers. Apply a dab of glue on each end. Pinch it on one side of the boot (see Fig 3.23). Repeat with the other side.

13 Hold the toe of the boot in one hand and the heel in the other. Pinch the two ends toward each other to form a slight arch. Touch up the edges with a matching color pen. If you wish, add decorative stitching with a felt-tip marker pen in a contrasting color.

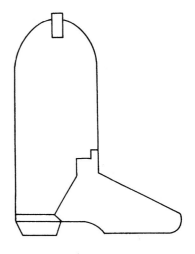

FIG 3.23

Nostalgic

Tissue flowers ★ LP record and album cover

Slinky™ ★ Coloring book ★ Crayons

Black light poster ★ Blue jeans

Beanbag chair ★ Lincoln Logs™ and container

Aluminum Christmas tree

Nostalgia a longing for something far away and long ago
(Webster's New Universal Unabridged Dictionary)

In 1976, to acknowledge the role of Levi's® jeans in clothing history, the Smithsonian Institute in Washington DC added a pair to its permanent collection. Arguably the world's favorite brand, antique Levi's® jeans are highly collectible and fetch high prices

As we age, we reflect on the golden times of our youth and the objects that were significant during that period. We want to relive our memories through these objects.

This desire to revisit specific moments of the past is compelling in American culture. The phrase 'everything old is new again' is being used in relation to items such as kids' toys and cars. Compare today's teen fashions with the 1970s originals and it is hard to distinguish between them.

Antique has become chic. What was once discarded or viewed as utilitarian is in demand. Collectors and ordinary folks alike are willing to pay high prices for everyday items. Nostalgia is hot.

Baseball trading cards are a good example of the trend. Kids once collected them to track the team affiliation of a favorite player. If the player was traded to another team, many would scratch out the name of the player's old team and write the name of the new one on the card. If a player fell out of favor, the baseball card served another purpose: it was folded in half and clipped to the spokes of a bicycle with a clothes pin. As the rider rode down the street, the card made a clicking sound.

What has contributed to the rise in nostalgia? The baby boom generation. Born after World War II, this group is responsible for defining everything from trends in fashion to must-have high-tech gadgets. As they reach

middle age, they look back with soft-focused affection on their youth. This has led to a resurgence in interest in the items of the recent past: beanbag chairs, sports trading cards, Beatles and Elvis Presley records, and movie memorabilia.

With large disposable incomes, the boomers are prepared to pay high prices for authentic items. A single 1952 Mickey Mantle baseball card, which originally sold for 5 cents in a package with a stick of gum, recently sold at auction for $121,000. Today, many parents have serious regrets over throwing out Junior's collection of trading cards and toys.

Much of the recent resurgence of interest in the past is media-related. Reruns of TV shows from the 1950s and 1960s, and advertisements featuring pieces of music or lyrics from the period contribute.

Will our desire to revisit the golden age of our pasts ever pass? It is unlikely; it serves to fend off present-day concerns and keeps alive memories of happier times.

'I Love Lucy' was first aired in the 1950s. Its star, Lucille Ball, is a much-loved American icon

Tissue flowers

Tools and materials

Brightly colored tissue paper
Fine-gauge craft wire
Large bead for vase
Scissors
Wire cutters
Needle-nose pliers

These simple flowers will never wilt or die or cause an allergic reaction: they are crafted from pieces of tissue paper.

Tissue flowers were popular during the 1970s. For a few cents, a creative college student could turn bunches of tissue paper into blossoms and add splashes of color to a drab room.

The tissue paper's weight gives the flowers a translucent quality. It is easy to shape and inexpensive to replace, and comes in a multitude of colors: fuchsia, orange and lime, to match the trendy colors of the era.

Use these miniature tissue flowers to decorate a retro scene or display in a Mexican home or market.

Finished size

Each flower, including stem, is 1³/₄in (4.5cm) high and ³/₄in (2cm) in diameter

METHOD

1 For each brightly coloured flower, cut six sheets of tissue paper into 1in (2.5cm) squares.

2 Cut a piece of fine wire 3in (7.6cm) long for the stem. This will later be inserted into a vase.

3 Stack the tissue paper squares. Carefully fold the squares accordion or fan style (see Fig 4.1). Each fold should be about ¹/₈in (0.25cm) in width. You should be able to make seven or eight folds.

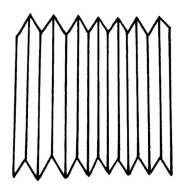

FIG 4.1

4 Fold the stack of tissue paper squares in half. Wrap the wire around the stack. Twist the wire around the stack with needle-nose pliers (see Fig 4.2).

5 Separate the tissue into individual petals (see Fig 4.3A).

6 Fluff up the flower into shape by gently pulling up on the petals with your fingertips (see Fig 4.3B).

7 Make five (or more) flowers and twist the stems together. Place them in a decorative bead vase for a splash of color.

FIG 4.2

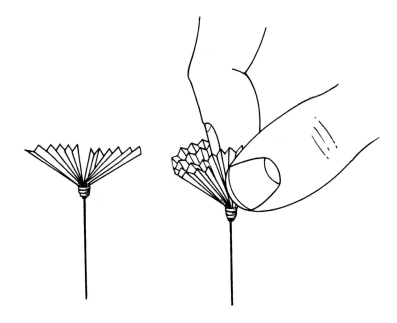

FIG 4.3A   FIG 4.3B

LP record and album cover

Tools and materials

Card (black/white or colored)

Photocopy paper (white)

Image (for cover)

Pair of sharp scissors or craft knife

Circular template, $^{15}/_{16}$in (2.4cm)

$^1/_4$in (0.5cm) hole punch

Metal straight-edged ruler

Square

Pencil

Paintbrush

Needle

PVA glue

Decoupage solution or water-based acrylic varnish

Finished size

LP is $^{15}/_{16}$in (2.4cm) in diameter

Cover is $1^1/_{16}$in (2.7cm) square

What teenager has not been told to 'turn that music down!' by a near-deaf parent? Today's teens annoy their parents just as much as the teens of the 1960s and 1970s who cranked up their stereos to listen to LPs.

'LP' means 'long play' which became synonymous for music recorded on large vinyl discs. These records were also known as $33^1/_3$s: the number of revolutions per minute (rpm) the record spun on the turntable. The first LPs offered 20 minutes of music per side, whereas the 78 rpm of earlier recordings only contained 4 to $4^1/_2$ minutes of music per side. The smaller 45 rpms held even less music than their 78 rpm cousins: approximately 3 minutes' worth.

LPs were sold in album covers to protect them from dust and scratches. The covers also provided information about the music and candid photographs of the performers.

Selecting the art for the cover was as essential as choosing the songs for the album. In 1939, Alex Steinweiss designed the first modern album cover for Columbia Records and changed the way records were marketed and sold almost overnight.

The cover became a critical marketing tool and many evolved into works of art. Artist Peter Max, known for his fantastical paintings of the 1970s, created the cover artwork for several major pop groups.

The Recording Industry of America awards gold and platinum records to musicians who sell a specific number of records. Artists who sell 500,000 receive a gold record to commemorate the event. Those whose records (45s, too) achieve 1,000,000 sales receive a platinum replica.

No need to worry about cracking or warping this miniature LP record. Add the LP and album cover to a teen's bedroom, or stack a bunch of albums together in a record store scene.

METHOD

LP RECORD

1 Apply three or four coats of varnish to both sides of a piece of black card. You will need to coat an area about 1¹⁄₂in (3.8cm) square. Allow each coat to dry thoroughly before applying another.

2 Punch out two circles from the white photocopy paper using the hole punch.

3 Place the ¹⁵⁄₁₆in (2.4cm) circular template onto the varnished card. Run a pencil several times around the template to make the circle and carefully cut out with a pair of scissors or craft knife (see Fig 4.4).

FIG 4.4

4 Punch a hole in the center of the black card circle with a needle. Punch a hole in the center of each ¹⁄₄in (0.5cm) white paper circle. Glue one ¹⁄₄in (0.5cm) white paper circle to each side of the black card circle using the needle to match up the holes (see Fig 4.5). Enlarge the hole slightly by pushing the needle through all three layers.

FIG 4.5

ALBUM COVER

1 Cut a strip of white or colored card 1¹⁄₁₆ x 2¹⁄₈in (2.7 x 5.4cm). Mark the center at 1¹⁄₁₆in (2.7cm). Score the card with the back of a craft knife at the center line. Fold the strip in half lengthwise. Apply a thin line of glue along two edges. Leave one edge open. Press firmly.

2 Glue a 1¹⁄₃₂in (2.6cm) square picture cut from a magazine to the album cover for the cover art.

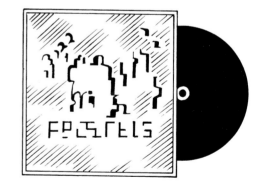

FIG 4.6

3 Insert the LP into the album cover (see Fig 4.6). Allow a little more than half of the LP to peep out. Glue in place if desired.

Slinky™ spring toy

Tools and materials

28-gauge craft wire, 6in
  (15cm) long
Wood dowel, ¹⁄₁₆in (0.1cm)
  in diameter
Wire cutter
Large needle

Jay Leno, stand-up comedian and host of *The Tonight Show*, once quipped that the Slinky™ is the only toy that encourages kids to play on the stairs.

The Slinky™ spring toy is an adaptation of a manufacturing part. In 1945, Richard T. James, a naval engineer, was inspecting a ship in a dockyard in Philadelphia. During his inspection a torsion spring fell off a table. The spring's bouncing motion gave James an idea. He decided to see if he could make a spring that 'walked'.

After much trial and error, James came up with a product which his wife dubbed a Slinky™. After a demonstration at a department store, James had a hit. In just 90 minutes, he sold 400 Slinkys.

The Slinky™ is made out of 88 coils of steel wire. Unwound, it is 69ft long. It moves down the stairs propelled by gravity and force.

James patented the toy and formed James Industries to manufacture it. To date, over 300 million have been sold.

Drape a mini Slinky™ spring toy over the edge of a toy box.

METHOD

1 Cut a piece of wire 6in (15cm) in length.

2 Wrap the wire tightly around the needle approximately 25 times to form a spring.

3 Cut the wire close to the last loop.

4 Cut another piece of wire about 1in (2.5cm) in length. Insert the piece into the spring. This internal wire helps the Slinky™ hold its shape while bending. It can be removed after bending.

5 Bend the spring over a ¹⁄₁₆in wood dowel to form the Slinky™. Cut the internal wire close to the ends.

Finished size
³⁄₄in (2cm) long

Coloring book

For most of us, our first foray into art is a coloring book and a box of crayons and an instruction to 'color inside the lines'. The more creative (or possibly anarchistic) of us made the trees purple and ignored the lines whenever possible – and now have thriving careers in fine art!

Coloring books and crayons are still a great tool for keeping children quiet in the back seat of a car on a long trip, and completed work decorates many a grandparent's refrigerator.

This miniature coloring book will add an affectionate touch to a child's bedroom.

Tools and materials

Card (mustard yellow) (or white card painted mustard yellow)
Photocopy paper (white)
Metal straight-edged ruler
Small rubber stamp images
Stamp pad (black)
Colored pencils
Pencil
Stapler

METHOD

1 Cut a strip of card $1^1/_{16}$ x $2^1/_4$in (2.7 x 5.7cm) for the coloring book cover. Mark the center line. Score with the back of a craft knife and a metal straight-edged ruler, and fold in half.

2 Cut five or six strips of photocopy paper, 1 x 2in (2.5 x 5cm) long. Fold each strip in half.

3 Stamp an image on each half of the fold of the photocopy paper strips with a selection of small rubber stamps. Stamp only on one side of the photocopy paper so that the images do not bleed through. Choose the best for the open pages.

4 Stack the pages on top of one another to make a book. Center the stack onto the card cover. Carefully staple a single staple into the fold (or spine) of the book. Staple the book from the outside so that the prongs feature on the inside. Color in as many of the images as you like with colored pencils. Decorate the cover, too, with text or a further stamped image.

Finished size

Open coloring book: $1^1/_{16}$ x $2^1/_4$in (2.7 x 5.7cm)

Crayons

Tools and materials

Card (mustard yellow) (or white
  card painted mustard yellow)
Polymer clay (eg. Fimo) (red,
  blue, yellow and brown)
Craft knife
Metal straight-edged ruler
Pencil
Fine-tipped marker (green)
Ceramic tile or sheets of
  aluminum foil
PVA glue

Finished size

Each crayon: $1/2$ x $1/4$in
  (1.25 x 0.5cm) in size

During the late nineteenth century, wax crayons were used primarily in industry. But in 1903, Edwin Binney and Harold Smith developed a crayon that children could use, too. They mixed two basic ingredients: paraffin wax and a coloring agent, to create the Crayola™ brand crayon.

Binney and Smith are probably single-handedly responsible for encouraging the creativity of many budding artists. Since 1903, the company, now a division of Hallmark Cards, has produced over 100 billion crayons in more than 120 colors.

Display your box of crayons in a miniature classroom scene.

METHOD

CRAYONS

1 To make the crayons, begin by rolling five or six thin rolls of polymer clay, a little less than $1/16$in (0.1cm) in diameter. You can mix various colors together: blue and yellow for green, or yellow and red for orange. Make extra crayons in different colors to have strewn around the coloring book if you wish.

2 Bake according to manufacturer's instructions. With a craft knife, cut each to $1/2$in (1.25cm) in length.

CRAYON BOX

1 Copy the rectangular template (see Fig 4.7) onto the mustard yellow card. If you wish, use white card and paint it a similar shade of yellow. The template shown is not drawn to scale, so follow the measurements carefully. The rectangle should measure, in total, $7/8$ x $11/16$in (2.2 x 1.7cm) in length. Note: it is easier to work in the center of a piece of card than at an edge, in case you need more room.

2 Once you have completed Fig 4.8 and made the horizontal markings, see Fig 4.9 for the vertical markings.

3 Score along all of the marked lines using the back of a craft knife and a metal-edged ruler.

4 Cut out the card, using Fig 4.10 as a guide with a craft knife and metal-edged ruler.

5 Cut a small window out of the short ¹/₄in (0.5cm) section with a craft knife.

6 Carefully fold the long sides to form a box. Overlap the sides and secure with a line of glue.

7 Overlap the short ends and secure with a line of glue. Draw two diagonal lines using the green marker across the front of the box (see Fig 4.11). If you have an authentic reference for the Crayola™ crayon box, your decoration will be more realistic.

8 Dry-fit the crayons in the box. Remove, place a small dab of glue on the ends before returning them to the box.

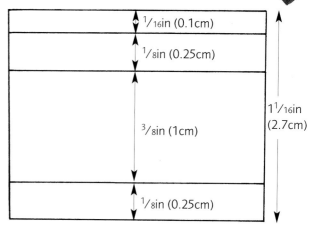

FIG 4.7

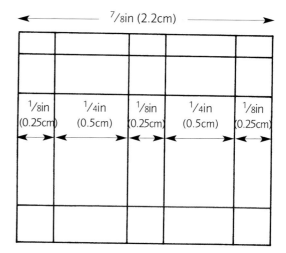

FIG 4.8

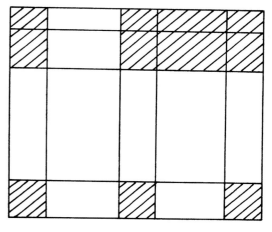

FIG 4.9

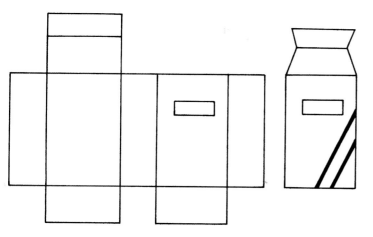

FIG 4.10   FIG 4.11

Black light poster

Tools and materials

Card

*Flocked paper (black) (from art
  and crafts stores)*

*3 or 4 fluorescent labels
  (different vibrant colors)*

Craft knife

Scissors

Metal straight-edged ruler

Circular template or compass

Finished size

2 x 3in (5 x 7.6cm)

When light is focused through a prism, it is broken down into visible colors: red, orange, yellow, green and indigo. Ultraviolet or black light lies beyond the blue end of the visible electro-magnetic spectrum and is invisible to the human eye. Bright or light-colored objects appear distorted when illuminated by a black light, and white objects take on an eerie glow.

Ultraviolet light became popular in the 1960s when young people discovered its unique properties on the posters featured in many teen bedrooms and on apartment walls. When lit by a black light, the images on the posters seemed to glow and move.

Hang this black light poster in your miniature teen bedroom or display it with other retro items like lava lamps and beaded curtains in a miniature shop.

METHOD

1 Cut a 2 x 3in (5 x 7.6cm) rectangle from both the card and flocked paper.

2 Cut the fluorescent labels into strips of various sizes. Apply the strips to the center section of the card (see Fig 4.12).

3 Draw a 1¾in (4.5cm) circle in the center of the back of the flocked paper. Draw a spiral within the circle, starting at the center (see Fig 4.13)

FIG 4.12

4 Cut along the spiral using a pair of sharp scissors to create a spring shape. Gently pull the spring away from the paper. Carefully trim around the spring, clipping off about ¹⁄₁₆in (0.1cm).

5 Fold the spring back down into the center of the circle. Lay the flocked side down on a clean sheet of photocopy paper. Apply glue sparingly to the back of the flocked paper and along the spiral.

6 Lay the card with the fluorescent strips face down over the back of the flocked paper. Press lightly into place.

FIG 4.13

Blue jeans

Blue jeans have become the epitome of style. The uniform of youth, they are everywhere: from boardroom to backroom.

Arguably the most famous brand of blue jeans in the world is Levi's® jeans. More than just a brand name, Levi's® jeans honor the inventor of the pants, 'Loeb' Levi Strauss, a 24-year-old Bavarian who emigrated to the US in the nineteenth century.

During the gold rush days of the 1850s, Strauss opened a wholesale dry goods business in San Francisco. Strauss had traveled west to sell canvas for tents and wagons, but switched to clothing when the miners needed sturdier work pants. Over the next 20 years, he built up a successful business.

One of his customers was a tailor named Jacob Davis. Davis had a customer who kept ripping the pockets out of his denim pants. His solution was to install copper rivets at the stress points in the pants. However, without money to patent the idea, Davis approached Strauss about a joint business partnership, which is why the patent for riveted jeans is in both men's names.

The Levi Strauss & Co. celebrates May 20, 1873 as the 'birthday' of blue jeans. While denim pants had been around for many years, the rivets engendered a new fashion trend.

Tools and materials

6in (15cm) square piece of thin denim

Thread (blue, non-metallic gold)

Fusible web fabric (eg. Wonder-Under by Pellon) (optional)

Scissors

Needle

Iron

Dressmaker's pins

Metal straight-edged ruler

Craft knife

Sewing machine (optional)

Fabric glue

Fray Check (optional)

Finished size

3¹/₁₆in (7.8cm) in length

> **NOTE**
>
> **The jeans are sewn in an unconventional manner, which you may find works well for miniatures. They are sewn using a ¹/₄in (0.5cm) seam allowance.**

Traditional blue jeans are made from denim. Some believe that 'denim' is an English corruption of the French 'serge de Nimes', a fabric from Nimes in France. But serge de Nimes was made of silk and wool while denim is made from cotton. So, the jury is still out on the origin of denim. Also a mystery is the origin of the word 'jeans'. It might be a derivation of 'Genoese', referring to the pants worn by sailors from Genoa, Italy.

The oldest pair of Levi's® jeans is held in the Levi Strauss & Co. Archives in San Francisco. Discovered in 1948 in an abandoned silver mine in California's Mojave Desert, they have been dated to around 1890. To acknowledge their enduring role in clothing history, the Smithsonian Institute in Washington, DC, added a pair of Levi's® jeans to its permanent collection in 1976.

These miniature blue jeans are versatile. They can be displayed either hanging in the closet of a teenager's bedroom, draped over a bed, or tucked into a miniature pile of laundry. Alternatively, why not add them to a Western scene?

METHOD

1 Trace the pattern (see Fig 4.14) onto the lightweight denim fabric. Cut two pieces.

2 With right sides facing, sew along one of the long sides in blue thread. Press seam open, trim the threads and then the seam.

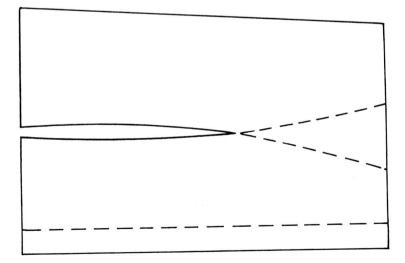

FIG 4.14

3 Refer to Fig 4.15. With the wrong side up, press the fabric down $1/2$in (1.25cm) along the top. Top stitch (regular machine stitch or hand stitch) the denim on the right side with gold thread for the waistband. Press and trim threads.

4 With wrong side up, press up $3/8$in (0.2cm) at the bottom of leg sections to form a hem. Top stitch on right side with gold thread. Press and trim the threads.

FIG 4.15

5 With right sides together, stitch a dart at the center of the rear seat with blue thread. Press to one side and trim.

6 With right sides together, stitch along the remaining long side. Press seam open. Trim seam and threads.

7 With right sides together, pin around the inside legs and sew with blue thread. Finger press seams open. Trim seams and threads. (See Fig 4.16.) Turn jeans right side out.

FIG 4.16

8 Press the jeans flat. Make a reverse dart in front to form the fly. Handstitch a cross with gold thread to represent a button, securing the fly at the waist. Make two tiny stitches through all layers close to the crotch.

9 Iron a piece of fusible web to the wrong side of a scrap of denim. Cut a strip $1/8$in (0.25cm) wide with a craft knife, using a metal ruler as a guide. (Optionally, use Fray Check instead of fusible web.) Let the fabric dry thoroughly before cutting.

10 Cut the fused strip of denim into four $1/2$in (1.25cm) sections for the belt loops. Apply a dab of glue to one end of one of each strip to form the loops. Attach them just above the top stitching on the waistband at intervals. Place another dab of glue on the opposite ends. Fold the ends over. Attach the opposite ends to the inside of the waistband. If this process is fiddly, you can use a needle to help create the loops.

Beanbag chair

Tools and materials

*Lightweight denim or alternative
  cotton fabric*

Matching thread

Sand (for filling)

Scissors

Dressmaker's pins

Sewing machine

Needle

Funnel

Iron

Fabric glue

Finished size

$2^{3}/_{4}$in (7cm) in diameter

A piece of hide filled with hair, feathers or seeds was possibly the ancient precursor to a ball. Part of this beanbag toy's charm may have been the noise it made when tossed in the air or the 'scrunchy' sensation when caught in the palm of the hand.

From a simple ball, the beanbag evolved into a game. Players acquired points by throwing the bags at a board filled with holes, the object being to get the bags through the holes with the highest number of points.

In the late 1960s and early 1970s, the beanbag was transformed from a toy into a trendy piece of furniture. In 1969, Italian designers Piero Gatti, Cesare Paolini and Franco Teodor developed the Sacco chair, mass-produced by Zanotta. The chair: a large, sealed bag, was filled with millions of tiny polystyrene balls.

Part of the chair's appeal was the way in which it molded to an individual's shape. It was often made of a type of canvas, but sometimes leather or *faux* fur. The chairs occasionally came with zippers that allowed the sitter to add polystyrene balls or remove some to make it softer.

The chair's accessible price, level of comfort and funky style made it a staple in a college dorm room or a first apartment.

Make a beanbag chair for your miniature apartment.

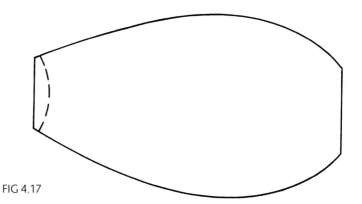

FIG 4.17

METHOD

1 Trace the pattern onto a piece of fabric. Cut out six pieces.

2 With right sides together, sew the sections using a ¼in (0.5cm) seam allowance to form a ball (see Figs 4.18 and 4.19). Press the seams with your fingers. Trim them closely.

3 Sew along the narrow end to close. Turn the ball right side out.

4 Fill the ball about a quarter of the way with sand, using a funnel if necessary. Slip stitch the bottom closed.

5 Cut a further 1½in (3.8cm) circle from the fabric. Sew a running stitch ¼in (0.5cm) from the edge around the circle with the needle and thread. Pull on the thread ends to create a ¾in (2cm) circle with finished edges. Press flat. Glue the circle to the bottom of the chair to cover the stitching underneath.

FIG 4.18

FIG 4.19

109

Aluminum Christmas tree

Tools and materials

Wood dowel, $^3/_{32}$in (0.2cm) in
   diameter, 6in (15cm) long

Pipe cleaners (silver)

Miniature wooden flower pot,
   $^1/_2$in (1.25cm) high

BBs or sinkers (small, lead
   fishing weights)

Card or cardboard

Fine-grade sandpaper

Acrylic paint (metallic silver)

Wire cutter

Pin vise and small drill bit

Paintbrush

Pencil

PVA glue

Finished size

7in (16.5cm) tall

It is said that German theologian Martin Luther is responsible for founding the tradition of the Christmas tree. During a walk in the woods one evening, he was inspired by the stars that appeared to sit on the branches of a fir tree. He cut it down and brought it home, lit candles to simulate stars and used the tree to teach a lesson about everlasting life.

When German immigrants settled in the New World, the custom of the Christmas tree came along with them. Other non-German households soon adopted the tradition, too.

Over the years, the Christmas tree has undergone a transformation. Today's trees are often artificial – even fiber optic. And the post-war aluminum Christmas tree has returned with renewed popularity.

Post-World War II style was very deliberately 'modern'. In the late 1950s, the Christmas tree went from natural evergreen to silvery aluminum, and was available in a diverse range of sizes and textures. The only resemblance the aluminum tree had to its authentic green cousin was its cone shape.

Because the heat from fairy lights could potentially damage the man-made branches, many families decorated the tree using a color wheel: a multi-segmented ring of colored cellophane. It was fixed in front of a motorized floodlight and rotated, to dazzling effect. The silver tree was transformed by a rainbow of alternating colors: red, blue, green and yellow.

The aluminum tree fell out of favor, but today, there's a resurgence of interest in 1950s items and they are back in demand. Collectors scour antique and secondhand shops, willing to pay high prices. Manufacturers are even making them again for those who want to capture the spirit of the era.

The miniature aluminum Christmas tree can be used to decorate a 1950s or 1960s living room.

METHOD

1 Measure ½in (1.25cm) up from one end of the dowel and mark with a pencil. Make further marks every ⅛in (0.25cm), and draw rings around the dowel at each mark.

2 Drill a hole in the center of the top of the dowel with the pin vise and small drill bit. The hole should be approximately ¹⁄₁₆in (0.1cm) deep.

3 Drill a hole three-quarters of the way through the dowel starting with the first ring on the bottom. Turn the dowel a one-quarter turn. Drill a hole in the center of the next ring (see Fig 4.21). Continue turning the dowel in one-quarter turns in a spiral fashion, drilling 43 holes in all (see Fig 4.20).

FIG 4.20

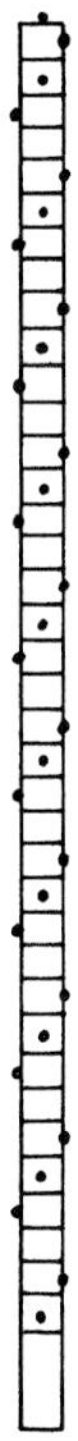

FIG 4.22

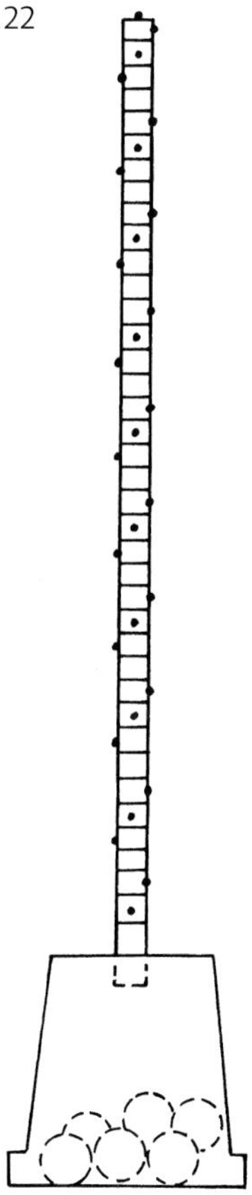

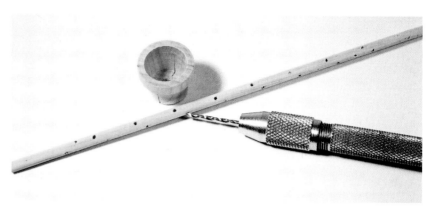

FIG 4.21

NUMBER OF PIPE CLEANERS	LENGTH
9	2in (5cm)
8	1¾in (4.5cm)
6	1¼in (3.8cm)
6	1¼in (3.2cm)
6	1in (2.5cm)
6	¾in (2cm)
5	½in (1.25cm)
3	¾in (2cm) (for the top)

4 Sand any roughened edges. Next, paint the dowel and the outside of the flowerpot with silver paint.

5 Cut your pipe cleaners into the appropriate lengths, to a total of 46. See panel, left, for the correct dimensions.

6 Enlarge the hole on the bottom of the flowerpot if necessary to fit the dowel. Trace the top of the flowerpot onto a piece of card. Cut out the card circle.

7 Invert the flowerpot. Glue the bottom of the dowel into the hole of the pot. Make sure the dowel is standing straight (see Fig 4.22, previous page). Allow to dry. Place some BBs or fishing weights in the flowerpot for ballast. Glue the card circle to the flowerpot.

8 Pour a pool of glue onto a scrap of paper. Starting with the longest pipe cleaners, dip the end of one of the long pipe cleaners into the glue. Twist it into the first hole at the bottom. Continue working your way up the dowel, inserting increasingly smaller pipe cleaners as you go. Allow to dry.

9 Twist the bottom of the three ¾in (2cm) sections together. Dip one end into the glue and attach this to the top of the dowel for a tree topper.

10 Once the glue has dried, shape the tree by bending the pipe cleaners up slightly.

Lincoln Logs™ and container

One of the most enduringly popular toys during the 1950s and 1960s was a set of Lincoln Logs™.

Owning a set of original Lincoln Logs™ encouraged budding architects and engineers to build their own pioneer settlements. It provided hours of creative play.

Named after Abraham Lincoln, the 16th president of the United States, who grew up in a log cabin in Kentucky, the toy was invented in 1916 by John Lloyd Wright, son of world-famous architect Frank Lloyd Wright.

Lincoln Logs™ were made from wood and stained to resemble the logs used in a full-size cabin. Each log had a flat top and a notched edge. This enabled them to stack and interlock without glue. Original sets came with red chimneys and green slats, which could be transformed into cabin roofs.

Children today can still receive a set of Lincoln Logs™ for Christmas. The product continues to be made by a private company in Pennsylvania and distributed by Hasbro, one of the world's leading toy companies.

Place a box, partially unwrapped, under your miniature Christmas tree, or display them disassembled in a child's bedroom.

METHOD

LOGS

1 To make the Lincoln Logs™ themselves, first cut the dowel into $^7/_{16}$in (2.2cm) lengths, preferably with a chopper (small hand axe). Create as many or as few as you like. Sandpaper smooth any rough edges.

2 For a little model, you will need two lengths sanded flat on one side. Run the section back and forth on the sandpaper about 20 times to create a flat side.

Tools and materials

LOGS
Wood dowel, $^1/_{16}$in (0.1cm) in diameter
Strip wood, $^3/_{16}$in (0.3cm) wide
Wood stain (redwood)
Acrylic paint (green)
Fine-grade sandpaper
Craft knife
Single-edged razor blade
Chopper (optional)
Paintbrush
PVA glue

STORAGE CONTAINER
Card (yellow)
Markers (green and brown)
Acrylic paint (green and silver)
Craft knife
Metal straight-edged ruler
Paintbrush
Marker or other round object, $^5/_8$in (1.6cm) in diameter
Circular template, $^5/_8$in (1.6cm) in diameter
PVA glue

Finished sizes
Logs: $^1/_{16}$in (0.1cm) in diameter and $^7/_8$in (2.2cm) long
Storage container: $^5/_8$in (1.6cm) in diameter

3 On each ⁷⁄₈in (2.2cm) length, mark a line ³⁄₁₆in (0.3cm) in from each end. Mark another line ³⁄₁₆in (0.3cm) beyond this one. Cut halfway through the dowel on each line with a single-edged razor blade. Remove the wood between the marked lines using the razor blade, shaving off the surface carefully away from you (see Fig 4.23). It is important that the cut-outs are in the same place on each piece so that your building is square.

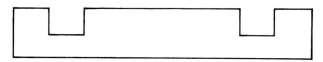

FIG 4.23

4 Cut a few lengths smaller than ⁷⁄₈in (2.2cm). Cut away ³⁄₁₆in (0.3cm) sections as in step 3 if desired. These sections can be strewn about as decoration rather than used in the construction.

5 When all sections have been cut, stain the pieces with wood stain and set aside to dry.

6 Cut the strip wood into 15 pieces, each 1in (2.5cm) long. Sand smooth any rough edges. Dilute some green acrylic paint with water and paint the strips. Set aside to dry.

7 Begin building a log cabin starting with the sections that you sanded flat. Make sure the first layer is perfectly square. Apply a dab of glue to the cut-out indentations to secure the layers. Build up two or three layers then place the other pieces around the building as though in progress.

CONTAINER

1 To make the storage container for the Lincoln Logs™, first cut a piece of card 1¹⁄₂ x 2³⁄₁₆in (3.8 x 5.5cm) in size. Color the top ¹⁄₄in (0.5cm) with a green marker as shown in the photograph. Write 'Lincoln Logs' in the green section with the brown marker. Draw logs on the yellow section (see Fig 4.24).

FIG 4.24

2 Draw two ⅝in (1.6cm) circles on the card. Cut out one circle on the exterior of the line. Cut out the other circle on the interior of the line.

3 Cut a piece of card ¹⁄₁₆in (0.1cm) wide and long enough to fit around the larger circle. Glue this strip around the outside edge of the larger circle to make the lid. Allow the glue to dry. Paint both sides of the lid with silver acrylic paint.

4 Wrap the decorated card around an object ⅝in (1.6cm) in diameter. Overlap the back edges. Test-fit the smaller circle on the bottom of the tube: it should just fit on the inside. Glue the back edge to secure the tube. Once the back is dry, glue the smaller circle to the inside of the tube bottom.

5 Fit the silver lid securely on the top of the tube.

Sporting

Baseball pennant  **Baseball hat**

Hot dog and bun ☆ **Table tennis paddles and ball**

Football ☆ **Basketball**

Bowling ball ☆ **Bowling bag** ☆ **Pizza**

Sports are an ingrained part of American culture, and a billion dollar business. TV companies compete for rights to televize games, agents negotiate huge sponsorship deals, and sports teams have extensive merchandizing.

Sport even has its own language. If you listen closely, you will notice that sporting terms have crept into the lexicon of American English. When a player takes 'time out', he or she is taking a break to discuss strategy with the coach. In parental language, time out means that a youngster has done something the parent does not like, and must spend some time alone to reflect on it. 'Scoring' – which is how one earns points in a game – has a very different connotation when applied to intimate relationships...

One reason why sport might be so popular is that it provides a connection between individuals that transcends race, religion, class, age or occupation. At sporting venues, it is not unusual to see laborers sitting next to corporate

A palatial sports stadium where Americans go to support their favorite teams

vice presidents, or senior citizens chatting with high school students.

To get an idea of the American obsession with sport, one need look no further than the palatial buildings built to house professional sports teams. A new baseball stadium recently opened in Milwaukee, Wisconsin, that cost over $400 million. Miller Park stadium comes equipped with a retractable roof and 'skyboxes' for those who can afford a more luxurious view.

Practising hard to become a great sports hero

Salaries of major sports figures regularly exceed $1 million. A Wisconsin football team, the Green Bay Packers, offered its star quarterback $101 million over a ten-year period. Companies pay $1 million for 30 seconds of television commercial time during play-off events such as the Super Bowl.

Many children dream of being a sports superstar, and that interest is often engendered from birth. New fathers give their sons rubber balls representing dad's favorite sport to play with. As kids grow older, parents sign their children up for a dozen sporting activities and spend hours attending competitions.

Perhaps unsurprisingly, sport even pervades the political arena. Media coverage of political elections and debates are often formatted to look like sporting events. And 'soccer moms' are considered a key group of voters by politicians. Sporting jargon such as winners, losers, scoring points, 'going on the offense' or 'playing defense' is all used in political speak, too, because the terms are so embedded in the public consciousness.

The game of baseball

Although the game is known as America's national pastime, baseball is likely derived from the British 'rounders'. The game of rounders has similar characteristics to its American cousin, but notable differences include calling a batter 'out' if he's hit with a ball and running the bases clockwise rather than counterclockwise.

Abner Doubleday is often considered the father of American baseball. He organized the first American baseball game, played in Cooperstown, New York, in 1839. But historians credit Alexander Cartwright with actually inventing the game. Cartwright replaced the softball with a harder one and instituted the practice of tagging rather than hitting the runner with the ball.

Baseball is played on a field that contains the following: three bases, a pitcher's mound and a home plate. Two teams of nine players alternate play during the game's nine innings. The team scoring the most points is declared the winner.

Each team has a pitcher, a catcher and seven fielders. All players bat in rotation. The pitcher's objective is to throw the baseball at the batter hoping he will swing at the ball with his bat and miss. If the batter swings and misses, and the ball was thrown within a certain zone, the batter earns a 'strike'. If the ball was thrown outside of the zone, the batter is awarded a 'ball'.

The American actress, Lynn Fontanne, was said to have observed after watching a baseball telecast: "I watched it for ever so long, ever so long, and finally I realized that the gentleman holding the bat is antagonistic to the gentleman holding the ball." Well said, Ms. Fontanne.

Three strikes and the batter is declared out; four balls and the batter can walk to first base. Three outs and the teams switch places, giving the outfield team a chance to earn points.

If the batter hits the ball, he runs to as many bases as he can before a player from the opposing team catches the ball. When an opposing player gets the ball, he throws it to a teammate on one of the bases. His teammate attempts to tag the batter with the ball before the batter touches base. If the batter is tagged, he's declared out. If the batter makes it around all the bases without getting tagged, he scores a home run and earns a point for his team.

Baseball pennant

Tools and materials

Flocked paper (various colors)
(from art and craft stores)
Plastic dowel, 1/16in (0.1cm)
in diameter
Gel pen (white or own choice
of color)
Scissors
PVA glue

Some die-hard baseball fans will do anything for the sport: attending games with their bodies painted the colors of their favorite teams, or sporting costumes that resemble the team's mascot. And team memorabilia often sells for hundreds – even thousands – of dollars.

Early last century, fans showed their support for their favorite teams during a game by waving triangular felt pennants attached to sticks. These were inscribed with the team's name and possibly its mascot and shaken when the favored team made a good play or to disagree with a referee's call.

1950s' and 1960s' youth collected pennants of their favorite teams, which decorated the walls of their bedrooms. Today, pennants are still sold as souvenirs, but many fans prefer to show their support by purchasing clothing with team logos.

Make several miniature pennants and mount them to the walls of a teenager's bedroom or fill a vendor's cart at a stadium.

Finished size

1⁷/₈in (4.7cm) wide

METHOD

1 Cut a rectangle, 2 x 1in (5 x 2.5cm) in size, diagonally in half into a triangle. Clip the top and bottom corners of the vertical side (see Fig 5.1).

FIG 5.1

2 Using a reference if you have one, copy your favorite team's name or mascot onto the pennant with the gel pen.

3 Cut the plastic dowel to a length of 2in (5cm). Fold over the clipped edge of the pennant to wrap around the dowel. Apply a small amount of glue. Press down firmly to secure.

Baseball hat

A baseball hat featuring the logo of a favored team is the standard uniform of many teens. The canvas hat sports a distinctive long bill in the front, vent holes on the top and an adjustable strap on the back.

Baseball players wear the hats to protect their eyes and head from the sun. They pull the hat down to a 90° angle with their eyebrows to avoid glare.

With pitchers throwing balls at speeds of over 100 mph, batters now wear heavy-duty plastic batting helmets instead of baseball hats when they bat. The helmets feature an extension to the side facing the pitcher to protect the player from a wayward ball.

The baseball hat has been appropriated by almost everyone: from outdoor workers to juvenile street gangs. Youths who wear certain colors, back-to-front or with the bill to one side do so to signal their gang affiliation.

Your miniature teenager should have a closetful of miniature baseball hats. Make a variety of hats in team colors.

Tools and materials

*Polymer clay (eg. Fimo) (blue or
  own choice of color)*
Acrylic paint (own color)
Craft knife
Paintbrush
*Ceramic tile or sheets of
  aluminum foil*
Oven

METHOD

1 Form the shape of the cap by rolling a ball of polymer clay, $^{1}/_{2}$in (1.25cm) in diameter. Flatten the ball with your fingers on one side to form the base of the cap. The front of the cap should be slightly higher than the back. Aim to create an approximate egg shape, slightly elongated to the rear.

2 Pinch out the front end to form the brim. This should extend in a raised curve approximately $^{3}/_{16}$in (0.2cm) out from the base of the cap.

3 Take a pinch of a matching or contrasting color clay and form the tiniest ball. Press this ball into the center top of the cap to form a button. Bake according to manufacturer's instructions and allow to cool.

Finished size
1 x $^{5}/_{8}$in (2.5 x 1.6cm)

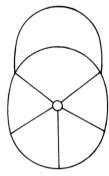

4 Score a line from side to side across the base of the brim with a craft knife to simulate the joint of brim to hat.

5 Create a 'stitched' seam by making a dotted line from the button to the base of the cap with a craft knife (see Fig 5.2).

6 Decorate your cap with the logo of your favorite team using a fine-tipped paintbrush.

FIG 5.2

Hot dog and bun

Tools and materials

Polymer clay (eg. Fimo) (brown, red, yellow and white)

Acrylic paint (yellow)

Chalk (brown)

Oven

Single-edged razor blade

Ceramic tile or sheets of aluminum foil

Cotton swab

Hairspray

Finished size

Hot dog in a bun is ³/₄ x ³/₈in (2 x 1cm)

Whether you call it a hot dog, a wiener, a frankfurter or a sausage, this well-loved American food is found in ballparks nationwide. There is even a National Hot Dog month every July.

In the 1860s, German immigrants were selling hot sausages from pushcarts in New York City. It was Thomas 'Tad' Dorgan, a cartoonist for *The New York Journal*, who coined the term 'hot dog'. During a chilly match at the New York Polo Grounds in 1901, the cold snacks were not selling well.

One of the vendors saw an opportunity and began selling sausages and rolls, calling them 'red hot dachshund sausages'. (Sausages were often referred to as dachshunds because of their resemblance to the long, skinny German breed of dog.) As he was completing his assignment for the paper, Dorgan couldn't spell the word dachshund and so wrote the words 'hot dog' in his cartoon of a barking sausage steaming in a roll. The term caught on and the rest is history.

The choice of toppings for hot dogs is extensive: mustard, ketchup, onions, pickles, relish or sauerkraut, or all of the above. And since you can never get too much of a good thing, some manufacturers produce a hot dog that is 1ft (30cm) long!

Your miniature family can buy a hot dog at a vendor's cart at a sports game or cook wieners in a backyard setting.

METHOD

1 For the hot dog, mix small pieces of half red, a quarter brown, and quarter yellow polymer clay. Shape the mixture into a snake-like roll ³⁄₄in (2cm) long and approximately ³⁄₃₂in (0.2cm) in diameter. Round off the ends. Bake according to manufacturer's instructions and allow to cool.

2 For the bun, mix brown and white polymer clay to resemble baked bread. Shape the clay mixture into a roll slightly longer than the hot dog and about the same diameter. Slice the bun on each side of the center to form a triangular-shaped wedge with a razor blade (see Fig 5.3). Carefully remove the wedge using the edge of the blade. Place the baked hot dog in the bun. Bake according to manufacturer's instructions and allow to cool.

3 Brush a thin line of yellow paint on top of the miniature hot dog to simulate mustard.

4 Brush the sides of the bun with a bit of brown chalk for realism, and lightly add hairspray to set.

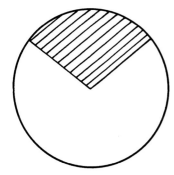

FIG 5.3

The game of table tennis

While the game of table tennis bears some resemblance to the full-scale version, it actually evolved from an indoor parlor game. Historians disagree about its origins, but during the late nineteenth century, it was played by the British upper class as an after-dinner diversion.

Table tennis was less energetic than regular tennis. And, once the meal was over and the dining room table cleared, guests could turn it into a game space.

Equipment manufacturers gave the game a lot of names: 'miniature tennis', 'whiff whaff', 'gossima' and 'flim flam'. But the US toy manufacturer, Parker Brothers, came up with the name Ping-Pong™, which stuck.

In 1971, the popularity of table tennis peaked in the US when the American team visited China, a country where the game is a national sport. US television coverage demonstrated that competition-level table tennis required great agility, stamina and speed.

The game is played on a table 9ft (2.7m) long by 5ft (1.5m) wide. The table bed stands 2½ft (0.75m) off the floor. Each end has 15ft (4.5m) of running room, which is why players need a lot of stamina to compete.

The object of the game is to be the first player to reach 21 points, with a two-point lead. If it is a close game, the players must continue to battle until one of them gains the two-point margin and wins. This leads to some long games!

Today, the popularity of the sport endures. The International Table Tennis Federation is now the world's largest sports federation and has 91 member nations.

Table tennis paddles and ball

The Ping-Pong™ ball is made from white plastic. Paddles are made of a flat piece of wood and can be any size, weight or shape. Display these paddles and ball in a family room or basement.

METHOD

1 For the Ping-Pong™ balls, roll balls of white polymer clay $^3/_{32}$in (0.2cm) in diameter. Bake in the oven and allow to cool.

2 For the paddles, cut two pieces of the wooden dowel $^1/_4$in (0.5cm) long. Sever the dowel in half lengthwise using a craft knife or razor blade. Push the knife or blade into the cut side of each half, $^3/_{32}$in (0.2cm) deep from the top edge. Whittle away the wood until you create an indentation halfway through the dowel (see Fig 5.5).

3 Apply a thin line of glue to the cut sides of the dowel. Glue the two halves of the dowel back together. Allow the glue to dry. Rub the cut sides of the dowel back and forth on a piece of fine-grade sandpaper to flatten.

4 Draw two $^7/_{16}$in (1.1cm) circles on a piece of card. Draw a small triangle on the bottom of each circle (see Fig 5.6) and cut out.

5 Paint the circles with acrylic green paint on both sides. Put to one side to dry.

6 Dry-fit the circles into the slots of the dowels. Trim the triangle if necessary. Apply a dab of glue to the base of the triangle. Attach the base of the triangle to the dowel.

7 Attach a Ping-Pong™ ball to one of the paddles with a dab of glue to display.

Tools and materials

Polymer clay (eg. Fimo) (white)
$^1/_8$in (0.25cm) wood dowel
$^1/_{32}$in (0.05cm) card
Acrylic paint (green)
Fine-grade sandpaper
Craft knife or single-edged blade
Paintbrush
Circular template, $^7/_{16}$in (1.1cm)
Scissors
Pencil
Metal straight-edged ruler
Ceramic tile or aluminum foil
PVA glue

Finished size

Paddles are $^3/_4$in (2cm) long
Ball is $^3/_{32}$in (0.2cm) in diameter

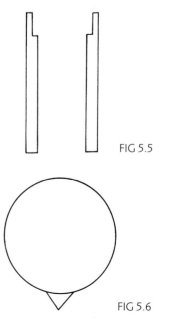

FIG 5.5

FIG 5.6

The game of football

Possibly the most dreaded phrase in the English language for many American women who are not themselves die-hard fans, is 'football season'. With its imminent approach, so-called 'football widows' start making alternate plans for companionship for the next five-and-a-half months.

The basic game consists of two teams of 11 men who try to move an 'oblate spheroid' (the ball) down the field to each other's goal line. While one team tries to get the ball to their side of the field (the offense), the other tries to stop them and take back the ball (the defense). Once the defense recovers the ball, they become the offense, and the game continues through four quarters of play.

A player must focus on several things at once: who has the ball, where the ball is on the field and how to overcome any blockages – ie. big players – from the other team coming between the player, the ball and the goal line. The player's aim is to keep hold of the ball and avoid being tackled by men from the opposite team who weigh more than a small horse.

The object of the game is to run or throw the ball so that it ends up on the offense's end of the field and thus score a touchdown (which is worth six points). After scoring a touchdown, the offense can then attempt to kick the ball through the goal posts to earn another point or run it over the goal line for two points. The team with the highest score at the end of the four quarters wins.

Football

In the early days of this game, the football was made from pigskin, which explains why many pre-game television shows are referred to as 'pigskin previews'. Cowhide is now the preferred material for the football.

A football contains an inflated rubber bladder, which helps it hold its shape. The ball weighs between 14 and 15oz (425g) and is 11in (28cm) long. A full-size ball is 7in (17.7cm) in diameter.

Your miniature football can be incorporated into a teen bedroom or displayed on a shelf in a garage or basement.

METHOD

1 Shape the football into an oval with a ball of brown polymer clay $^{11}/_{16}$in (1.7cm) in diameter. Work around the ball with your fingers to make the points at each end (see Fig 5.7).

2 Place the football in the center of the piece of aluminum foil. Crumple the corners of the foil to keep the ball from rolling while it is baking. Bake according to manufacturer's instructions, and allow to cool.

3 Score lines from end to end on the top, bottom and each side of the ball with a craft knife. If you have the genuine article to use as a reference, all the better.

4 Flatten the white polymer clay until paper-thin. Cut two strips less than $^{1}/_{16}$in (0.1cm) thick to make the football laces. Lift the strips with the tip of the craft knife. Lay the clay strips across the center of the top of the football lengthwise adjacent to each other.

5 Cut eight strips $^{1}/_{32}$ x $^{1}/_{4}$in (0.05 x 0.5cm). Lay these evenly spaced strips widthwise across the top of the other strips. Press lightly in place. Bake again for up to ten minutes.

Tools and materials

Polymer clay (eg. Fimo) (brown and white)
Aluminum foil, 3in (7.6cm) square
Craft knife
Ceramic tile or sheets of aluminum foil
Oven

Finished size
1in (2.5cm) long

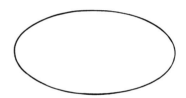

FIG 5.7

The game of basketball

It was a desire to keep students occupied during the cold winter months of 1891 at Springfield College in Massachusetts that led to the creation of a truly all-American sport: basketball.

Dr. James A. Naismith, a student at the all-male college, rose to a teacher's challenge to develop an indoor game that his peers would want to play. Naismith nailed a peach basket to the side of the balcony at each end of the college gymnasium, and had his classmates attempt to throw a soccer ball into it. Once the students got the ball in the basket, Naismith realized that he had to find a way to get it out. He recruited a janitor to sit on the top of a ladder and retrieve any balls that made it in the basket.

From these humble beginnings evolved a sport that, today, has kids consistently emulating their favorite players. Players such as Michael Jordan, Larry Bird and Ervin 'Magic' Johnson have become household names – heroes, even – with their own brands of sports clothes and shoes.

Basketball

Today's players, whether professional or amateur, use a regulation-sized leather ball and basket composed of a woven net attached to a metal ring.

A standard basketball is 9in (23cm) in diameter. Professional balls are made from leather, but balls used for nonregulation play can be made from rubber or synthetic materials.

The basketball's surface is textured to improve its grip. Fully inflated, it weighs between 20 and 22oz (600g), no problem for players who stand 7ft (2.1m) in height and whose hands are like baskets, too.

The ball is tossed into a metal ring called a hoop. The hoop holds the net, which slows down the ball as it passes through. The net also has a practical side: it allows the referees, the players and the fans to see that a basket has actually been made.

Place your miniature basketball on a court, in a garage or in a teenager's bedroom.

METHOD

1 Use orange polymer clay or create your own shade of orange by mixing small pieces of yellow, red and brown polymer clay together. The color of the basketball can range from bright to dark orange or brown. Shape the clay into a ball approximately $^3/_4$in (2cm) in diameter. Slightly flatten the ball on the most suitable side so that it sits on a surface without rolling. Bake according to manufacturer's instructions and allow to cool.

2 Sketch lines around the ball for the side seams with a pencil. There should be eight sections. Refer to Figs 5.8 and 5.9 for the patterns.

3 Fill in the seams by either drawing them very carefully with a permanent black marker or using the thread method.

4 To apply the thread method, score along the pencil lines with a craft knife. Make the cuts deep enough to hold a piece of thread. Use the tip of a needle to widen the lines if necessary.

5 Apply a thin line of glue into the scored lines. Attach a piece of black thread along the lines. Clip the ends and secure by pushing them into the groove with a needle. Be especially careful along the side seams so that the thread follows the curve. Repeat until the whole ball is threaded.

Tools and materials

Polymer clay (eg. Fimo) (orange or red, yellow, brown)
Thread (black) (optional)
Craft knife
Fine-tipped permanent marker (black)
Oven
Ceramic tile or sheets of aluminum foil
Pencil
Needle (optional)
PVA glue (optional)

Finished size

$^3/_4$in (2cm) in diameter

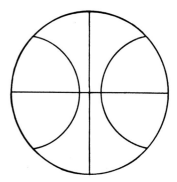

FIG 5.8

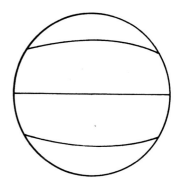

FIG 5.9

The game of bowling

In *Bowling Alone: The Collapse and Revival of American Community*, author Robert Putnam notes that while more Americans are bowling today than ever before, bowling in organized leagues has dropped precipitously in the last ten years. He found that between 1980 and 1993, the total number of bowlers in America increased by ten percent, while league bowling decreased by 40 percent.

While there seems to be a trend toward solo rather than team bowling, there's little concern that the sport will die out. After all, the game has conceivably been around for thousands of years. Items found in the tombs of the ancient Egyptians suggest that the pharaohs enjoyed a similar activity.

Bowling has always been a popular sport in working-class neighborhoods. The rise of the automobile and the invention of the automatic pin setter took the game to the suburbs, but it continues to retain its blue-collar fan base.

During the game, bowlers use an underarm throw to toss or roll a heavy ball down a varnished wooden alley in an attempt to knock down the ten wooden pins at the end. The pins are set in a pyramid formation. Points are scored based on how many pins are knocked down. A perfect score is 300. To achieve that, the bowler must knock down all ten pins every turn until the end of the game.

Bowling ball

Bowling balls are made from composite rubber and weigh between 10lbs (4.5kg) and 16lbs (7.3kg). Bowling alleys provide balls in a variety of weights for their customers, but nowadays many bowlers have their own customized balls.

When asked about the choice of color on his Model T cars, magnate Henry Ford was reported to have said, "You can have any color you want as long as it's black". Bowling alleys follow suit: the majority of bowling balls are black. But some bowlers assert their sense of individual style by having balls with rainbow colors and sensational patterns.

In the late nineteenth century, bowlers held the ball in both hands to roll it. Sometime later, holes were drilled through the surface so that the bowler could control its release and projection down the alley.

Make several bowling balls in different colors for your own miniature alley.

Tools and materials
Polymer clay (choice of colors)
Pin vise and drill bit
Oven
Ceramic tile or aluminum foil

Finished size
Each bowling ball is $^3/_4$in (2cm) in diameter

METHOD

1 Mix your choice of colors of polymer clay for a marbled effect or use a single color. If attempting to mix colors for a marbled effect, do not over-mix: you want to see the color streaks.

2 Roll the polymer clay into a ball $^3/_4$in (2cm) in diameter. Slightly flatten the clay on the bottom so that it sits without rolling.

3 Bake according to manufacturer's instructions and allow to cool.

4 Drill three holes in the shape of a triangle for the finger holes with a pin vise and small drill bit (see Fig 5.10).

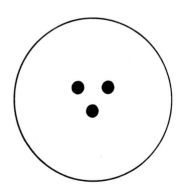

FIG 5.10

Bowling bag

Tools and materials

Thin leather/fabric-backed vinyl

Leather beading cord

Card

$^1/8$in (0.25cm) wood dowel

Heavy card, $^3/4$in (2cm) square

Gel pen (silver)

Very fine-tipped permanent
  marker (black)

Pair of sharp scissors

Craft knife

Circular template, $^3/4$in (2cm)

Metal straight-edged ruler

Square

Pencil

PVA glue

With a zippered top and handles, bowling bags carry the ball to and from the bowling alley. They come in many colors.

Fill your miniature bowling bag with a matching ball.

METHOD

1 Copy the template (see Fig 5.11), carefully following the measurements provided.

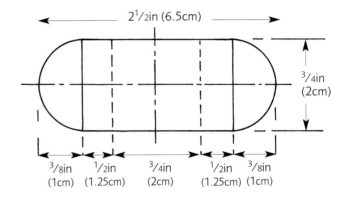

2½in (6.5cm)

$^3/4$in
(2cm)

$^3/8$in $^1/2$in $^3/4$in $^1/2$in $^3/8$in
(1cm)   (1.25cm)   (2cm)   (1.25cm)   (1cm)

FIG 5.11

2 Glue the pattern to the wrong side of the leather with the pattern facing upward. Cut out along the outside lines.

3 Score down the two lines of dashes using the blunt edge of a craft knife.

Finished size

With handles, the bowling bag
  is about $^3/4$in (2cm) wide by
  1in (2.5cm) high

4 Glue a $^3/4$in (2cm) square of heavy cardboard to the center section.

5 Cut a $^1/2$in (1.25cm) piece from the dowel. Fold up the two rounded ends of the leather. Glue the dowel at the points where the center line meets the top of the rounded ends (see Fig 5.12). Hold the rounded ends together until the glue sets. It should form a flat-topped triangle.

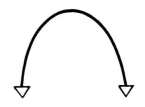

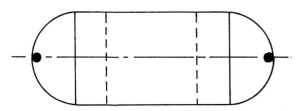

FIG 5.12

FIG 5.13

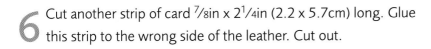

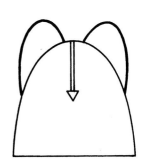

FIG 5.14

6 Cut another strip of card $^7/_8$in x $2^1/_4$in (2.2 x 5.7cm) long. Glue this strip to the wrong side of the leather. Cut out.

7 Apply a thin line of glue along the outside edges of the bag. Starting from the base of one side, glue the $^7/_8$in (2.2cm) strip of card to the bag. Keep the rounded top in the center of the strip. Allow the glue to dry.

8 Cut the strip along the edges of the bag with a pair of small sharp scissors. Be careful to cut the strip and not the bag itself.

9 Cut two pieces of leather beading cord $2^1/_4$in (5.7cm) long. Dry-fit the cord along the two cut edges of the bag. Trim if necessary. Apply a thin line of glue along the cut edge and attach the cord.

10 Cut two pieces of leather cord 1in (2.5cm) long. Fold the cord over slightly to form a handle. Cut four tiny triangles from the leather. Attach the triangles to the ends of the cord with a drop of glue (see Fig 5.13).

11 Glue one handle to each long side of the bag, about $^3/_4$in (2cm) up from the bottom.

12 For the zipper, draw a line down the center of the top of the bag with a silver gel pen. This should run from about $^3/_4$in (2cm) up from the bottom of each side. Once the gel dries, make lines from side to side on the zipper with a fine-tipped black marker.

13 Cut two more tiny triangles from the leather. Glue the triangles on each side with the points facing down at the base of the zipper (see Fig 5.14).

Pizza

Tools and materials

Polymer clay (eg. Fimo) (brown,
   translucent, red, yellow
   and white)
Acrylic varnish (satin)
Acrylic paint (yellow and red)
Chalk (brown)
Hairspray
Toothpick
Oven
Single-edged razor blade
Ceramic tile or sheets of
   aluminum foil
Mixing cup
Cotton swab, or bud

Finished size

1¹⁄₄in (3.2cm) in diameter

Historical records suggest that ancient Egyptians, Greeks and Romans all ate the forerunner of today's pizza: flat bread topped with olive oil, herbs and spices. The modern pizza is thought to have originated from seventeenth-century Naples. Brought to the US by Italian immigrants, it is now a staple of American cuisine.

To pass the test of the Associazione Verace Pizza Napoletana (the Association of Real Neapolitan Pizza), an authentic pizza must adhere to rigorous standards. The dough must be made only with flour, natural yeast or brewer's yeast, salt and water. It must be kneaded by hand or in a special mixer. It must be baked in a special wood-fired brick oven heated to at least 750° Fahrenheit. It is inserted and retrieved with a long-handled wooden paddle called a 'peel'.

Mozzarella cheese has been around since the seventh century. The people of India made it from the milk of water buffalo. It arrived in Italy during the eighteenth century.

Tomatoes were a later addition. When Christopher Columbus brought them back from the New World, they were thought to be poisonous! Some brave soul realized they were edible and Neapolitans soon began using them on their pizzas.

Today, Americans eat 100 acres of pizza each day (or 350 slices per second). Pepperoni is America's favorite topping, and thin crust is the favored base.

Add this miniature pizza to a kitchen or party vignette.

METHOD

1 For the pizza crust, mix small pieces of brown and white polymer clay until you achieve a color resembling baked bread. Flatten the clay mixture and shape it into a crust 1¹⁄₄in (3cm) in diameter. Build up the edges slightly. Bake according to manufacturer's instructions and allow to cool.

2 For the chopped onions, first shape a piece of translucent clay into a 1 x $\frac{1}{16}$in (2.5 x 0.1cm) rectangle. Bake according to manufacturer's instructions. Once cool, chop into onion slivers. Put these to one side.

3 For the mushrooms, combine small pieces of the following mix of polymer clay: one-third translucent, one-third brown, one-sixth white and one-sixth black. Do not over-mix: aim to achieve natural-looking streaks. Roll the mixture into a snake, $\frac{1}{8}$in (0.25cm) in diameter. Cut out two quarter sections using a blade to form the stem and cap (see Fig 5.15). Bake according to manufacturer's instructions. Once cool, slice into very thin pieces.

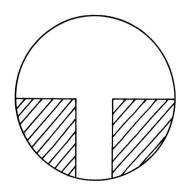

FIG 5.15

4 For the pepperoni, combine small pieces of the following colours for the right shade of orange: two-thirds red and one-third yellow. Make 25 very thin rolls with the mixture. Make five very thin rolls from the translucent polymer clay. Layer the rolls (see Fig 5.16). Make sure that the exterior rolls are all orange. Roll the layered rolls into one, $\frac{1}{8}$in (0.25cm) in diameter. Bake according to manufacturer's directions. Once cool, slice the large roll into paper-thin slices using a single-edged blade (see Fig 5.17). Allow some of the slices to curl slightly.

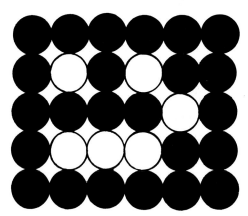

FIG 5.16

5 For the tomato sauce, mix a small amount of yellow and red acrylic paint together into an appropriate red. Paint the inside of the crust with the tomato red paint. Leave a tiny border of crust showing all the way around. Allow to dry.

6 For the cheese, add one or two drops of yellow acrylic paint to a small amount of acrylic satin varnish in a small mixing cup. Spread this mixture on top of the tomato sauce with a toothpick.

7 To assemble: before the varnish mixture dries, sprinkle the onion, mushrooms and pepperoni on top of the pizza. Add more 'cheese' if necessary. Allow to dry.

FIG 5.17

8 Make the final finishing touches. Lightly brush brown chalk around the edges of the pizza to darken the crust. Set the chalk by spraying lightly with hairspray.

Sources of Information

ORGANIZATIONS
North America
National Association of Miniature Enthusiasts
(NAME)
PO Box 69
Carmel, Indiana 46032
Tel: (317) 571–8094
Email: name@miniatures.org
Website: www.miniatures.org

International Guild of Miniature Artisans (IGMA)
PO Box 2320
Malta, New York 12020
Tel: (800) 711–IGMA (4462)/(518) 885–5744
Fax: (518) 885–2543
Website: www.igma.org

Miniatures Industry Association of America
(MIAA)
PO Box 3388
Zanesville, Ohio 43072
Tel: (614) 452–4541
Email: miaa.info@offinger.com
Website: www.miaa.com

Cottage Industry Miniaturists Trade
Association Inc. (CIMTA, Inc.)
PO Box 42849
Evergreen Park, Illinois 60805
Tel: (773) 233–5522
Fax: (773) 233–5506
Website: www.cimta.org

The National Polymer Clay Guild
Suite 115–345
1350 Beverly Road
McLean VA 22101

UK
The British Polymer Clay Guild
Great Wacton Hop Kilns
Bredenbury
Bromyard
Herefordshire, HR7 4T9
Tel: 01885–483275
Website: www.heaser.demon.co.uk

PUBLICATIONS
North America
Miniature Collector
801 W. Norton Avenue
Suite 200
Muskegon, MI 49441
Tel: (231) 733–9382
Fax: (231) 733–7635
Website: www.scottpublications.com

Dollhouse Miniatures
21027 Crossroads Circle
Waukesha, Wisconsin 53187
Tel: (800) 446–5489/(262) 796–8776
Website: www.dhminiatures.com

International Dolls' House (US)
Wise Owl Worldwide Publications
4314 W. 238th Street
Torrance, California 90505
Tel: (310) 375–6258

Dolls' House World (US)
Ashdown Publishing
227 Tebbs Avenue
Greendale, Indiana 47025
Tel: (812) 537–3335
Fax: (812) 537–9706
Email: hmp@one.net

UK
Dolls' House Magazine
166 High Street
Lewes
East Sussex
BN7 1XU
Tel: 01273–477374
Fax: 01273–402489
Email: christiane@thegmcgroup.com

International Dolls' House (UK)
Tower Publishing
Tower House
Sovereign Park
Market Harborough
Tel: 01858–468811

Dolls' House World (UK)
Avalon Court
Star Road
Partridge Green
West Sussex
RH13 8RY
Tel: 01403–711511
Fax: 01403–711521
Website: www.ashdown.co.uk

MINIATURE EVENTS
North America
Philadelphia Miniaturia
Box 518
Langhorne, Pennsylvania 19047
Tel: (215) 702–7116
Website: www.philadelphiaminiaturia.com

Chicago International Miniatures Show
Tom Bishop Productions, Inc.
PO Box 8571
Coral Springs, Florida 33075
Tel: (954) 755–0373
Fax: (954) 755–5508
Email: BishopShow@aol.com

International Guild of Miniature Artisans Show
IGMA
Box 2320
Malta, New York 12020
Tel: (800) 711–IGMA (4462)/(518) 885–5744
Fax: (518) 885–2543
Website: www.igma.org

Dallas Dollhouse Miniature Event
American Museum of the Miniature Arts
2001 N. Lamar Street
Suite 100
Dallas, Texas 75202
Tel: (214) 969–5502

UK
The London Dolls' House Festival
25 Priory Road
Kew
Surrey TW9 3DQ
Tel: 020 8948 1892
Fax: 020 8332 2894
Email: tickets@dollshousefestiv.demon.co.uk

MUSEUMS
North America
American Museum of the Miniature Arts
2001 N. Lamar Street
Dallas, Texas 75202
Tel: (214) 969–5502
Fax: (214) 969–5997

Art Institute of Chicago
111 S. Michigan Avenue
Chicago, Illinois 60603
Website: www.artic.edu
This is the permanent home of part of the Thorne Rooms.

The Denver Museum of Miniatures,
Dolls and Toys
880 Gaylord Street
Denver, Colorado 80206
Tel: (303) 332–3704

Delaware Toy and Miniature Museum
PO Box 4053
Route 141
Wilmington, Delaware 19807
Tel: (302) 427–TOYS (8697)
Website: www.thomes.net/toys/

Museum of Miniature Houses
111 E. Main Street
Carmel, Indiana 46032
Tel: (317) 575–9466

Museum of Science and Industry
57th Street and Lake Shore Drive
Chicago, Illinois 60637
Tel: (773) 684–1414
Website: www.msichicago.org
*Permanent home of the Colleen Moore
Fairy Castle.*

Naples Museum of Art
5833 Pelican Bay Boulevard
Naples, Florida 34108
Tel: (800) 597–1900/(914) 597–0670
Website: www.naplesphilcenter.org
*Incorporates the Pistner Collection, The Kupjack
Rooms and the Denis Hillman Collection. Also on
long-term loan: Masters of Miniature.*

Phoenix Art Museum
1625 North Central Avenue
Phoenix, Arizona 85004-1685
Email: info@phxart.org
Website: www.phxart.org/thorne_mini.html
*Permanent home of another part of the
Thorne Rooms.*

Tee Ridder Museum
15 Museum Drive
Roslyn Harbor, New York 11576
Tel: (516) 484–9338
Website: www.nassaumuseum.org/art/ridder.html

Toy and Miniature Museum of Kansas City
5235 Oak Street
Kansas City, Missouri 64112
Tel: (816) 333–2055
Website: www.umkc.edu/tmm/

Washington Doll's House and Toy Museum
5236 44th St. NW
Washington, DC 20015
Tel: (202) 244–0024
Fax: (202) 237–1659

The Mildred M. Mahoney Dolls' House Gallery
657 Niagara Boulevard
Fort Erie,
Ontario, L2A 3H9
Canada
Tel: (905) 871–5833

Bibliography

Andrews, Edward Deming and Faith, *Shaker Furniture: The Craftsmanship of an American Communal Sect*, Dover Publications, Inc., New York, NY, 1964

Bial, Raymond, *One-Room School*, Houghton Mifflin Company, Boston, MA, 1999

Binney, Ruth (Ed), *The Origins of Everyday Things*, The Reader's Digest Association Limited, Pleasantville, NY, 1999

Blount Christian, Mary, *Hats Are for Watering Horses: Why the Cowboy Dressed That Way,* Hendrick-Long Publishing Co., Dallas, TX, 1993

Bradley, Glenn D., *Pony Express*, A.C. McClurg and Company, Chicago, IL, 1923

Brandt, Betty, *Special Delivery*, Carolrhoda Books, Minneapolis, MN, 1988

Burton, Bill (Ed), *The Sportsman's Encyclopedia*, Grosset and Dunlap, New York, NY, 1971

Bykofsky, Sheree and Fargis, Paul (Eds), *The New York Public Library Desk Reference*, The Stonesong Press, Simon and Schuster, New York, NY, 1989

Carmichael, Suzanne, *The Traveler's Guide to American Crafts East of the Mississippi: A Traditional and Contemporary Selection*, E.P. Dutton, New York, NY, 1990

Carmichael, Suzanne, *The Traveler's Guide to American Crafts West of the Mississippi: A Traditional and Contemporary Selection*, E.P. Dutton, New York, NY, 1990

Christensen, Karen and Levinson, David (Eds), *Encyclopedia of World Sport*, Oxford University Press, Oxford, England, 1996

Creekmore, Betsey B., *Traditional American Crafts: A Practical Guide to 300 Years of Methods and Materials*, Hearthside Press, New York, NY, 1968

D'Amato, Janet and Alex, *Indian Crafts*, Lion Press, New York, NY, 1968

Davenport Bradon, Allen (Ed), *The Family Creative Workshop #2*, Plenary Publications International, New York, NY, 1974

Davenport Bradon, Allen (Ed), *The Family Creative Workshop #6*, Plenary Publications International, New York, NY, 1974

Davenport Bradon, Allen (Ed), *The Family Creative Workshop #12*, Plenary Publications International, New York, NY, 1974

Davidson, Alan, *The Oxford Companion to Food*, Oxford University Press, Oxford, England, 1999

Davis, William C., *The American Frontier: Pioneers, Settlers and Cowboys, 1800–1899*, Salamander, Smithmark Publishers, New York, NY, 1992

Elkhort, Martin, *The Secret Life of Food: A Feast of Food and Drink History, Folklore and Fact*, Jeremy Tarcher, Los Angeles, CA, 1991

Encyclopedia Americana, Grolier, 1996

Facklam, Margery and Phibbs, Patricia, *Corn Husk Crafts*, Sterling Publishing Company, New York, NY, 1974

Fiarotta, Noel and Phyllis, *The You and Me Heritage Tree: Ethnic Crafts for Children*, Workman Publishing Company, New York, NY, 1976

Flandrin, Jean-Louis and Montanari, Massimo (Eds), *Food: A Culinary History from Antiquity to the Present*, Columbia University Press, New York, NY, 1996

Flood, Elizabeth Clair and Manns, William, *Cowgirls: Women of the Wild West,* Zon International, Santa Fe, NM, 2000

Francis, Richard, *Ann, the Word: The Story of Mother Lee, Female Messiah, Mother of the Shakers, the Woman Clothed with the Sun*, Arcade Publishing, New York, 2001

Freedman, Russell, *Cowboys of the Wild West*, Clarion Books, New York, NY, 1985

Gibbons, Gail, *The Post Office Book: Mail and How It Moves*, HarperCollins Publishers, New York, NY, 1982

Gorsline, Marie and Douglas, *North American Indians*, Random House, New York, NY, 1977

Graves, Thomas E. and Yoder, Don, *Hex Signs: Pennsylvania Dutch Barn Symbols and Their Meaning*, E.P. Dutton, New York, NY, 1989

Harvey, Marian, *Crafts of Mexico*, Macmillan Publishing Company, New York, NY, 1973

Hawkins, Nancy and Arthur, *The American Regional Cookbook: Recipes from Yesterday and Today for the Modern Cook*, Prentice-Hall, New York, NY, 1976

Hedgepeth, Don, *The Art of Tom Lovell: An Invitation to History*, The Greenwich Workshop, Greenwich, CT, 1993

Hinson, Dolores, A., *Quilting Manual*, Hearthside Press, New York, NY, 1966

Holland, Thomas W. (Ed), *More Boys' Toys from the Fifties and Sixties*, The Windmill Group, Sherman Oaks, CA, 1998

Horsham, Michael, *The Art of the Shakers*, Chartwell Books, Secaucus, NJ, 1989

Hovis, Ford (Ed), *The Sports Encyclopedia*, Praeger Publishers, New York, NY, 1976

Hoyt Goldsmith, Diane, *Pueblo Storyteller*, Holiday House, New York, NY, 1991

Ingalls Wilder, Laura, *Little House on the Prairie*, Harper and Row Publishers, New York, NY, 1953

Jaber, William, *Wheels, Boxes and Skateboards*, Drake Publishers, New York, NY, 1976

Kauffman, Sandra, *The Cowboy Catalog*, Clarkson N. Potter Publishers, New York, NY, 1980

Ketchum, Jr., William C., *The Catalog of American Collectibles*, Mayflower Books, New York, NY, 1979

Ketchum, William C., *Western Memorabilia Identification and Price Guide*, Avon Books, New York, NY, 1993

Knox, Gerald H. (Ed), *Better Homes and Gardens: Traditional American Crafts*, Meredith Corporation, Des Moines, IA, 1988

Kreighbaum, Ellen F. and Smith, Mark A. (Eds), *Sports and Fitness Equipment Design*, Human Kinetics, Champaign, IL, 1996

L. Edward, Purcell, *The Shakers*, Crescent Books, New York, NY, 1988

Langley Sommer, Robin, *"I Had One of Those": Toys of Our Generation*, Brompton Books Corporation, Greenwich, CT, 1992

Larkin, David and Sprigg, June, *Shaker Life, Work and Art*, Stewart, Tabori and Chang, Inc., New York, NY, 1987

Lauber, Patricia, *Cowboys and Cattle Ranching: Yesterday and Today*, Thomas Y. Crowell Company, New York, NY, 1973

Mather, Christine, *Native America Arts: Traditions and Celebrations*, Clarkson N. Potter Publishing, New York, NY, 1990

Matthews, Leonard J., *Pioneers and Trailblazers: Adventures of the Old West*, Derrydale Books, New York, NY, 1990

McCutchen, Marc, *The Writer's Guide to Everyday Life in the 1800s*, Writer's Digest Books, Cincinnati, OH, 1993

McDermott, Catherine, *Design Museum Book of the 20th Century*, Overlook Press, Woodstock, NY, 1997

McDowell, Bart, *The American Cowboy in Life and Legend*, National Geographic Society, Washington, DC, 1972

Meany, Janet and Pfaff, Paula, *Rag Rug Handbook*, Dos Tejedoras Fiber Arts Publications, St. Paul, MN, 1988

Menke, Frank G., *The Encyclopedia of Sports*, A.S. Barnes and Company, Cranbury, NJ, 1977

Milord, Susan, *Adventures in Art: Art and Craft Experiences for 7 to 14 Year Olds*, Williamson Publications, Charlotte, VT, 1990

Minor, Marz and Nono, *The American Indian Craft Book*, University of Nebraska Press, Lincoln, NE, 1972

Murdoch, Alfred A., *Cowboy*, Alfred A. Knopf, Inc., New York, NY, 1993

Panati, Charles, *The Browser's Book of Beginnings: Origins of Everything Under and Including the Sun*, Penguin Putnam Publishers, New York, NY, 1998

Peel, Lucy and Powell, Polly, *'50s and '60s Style*, Chartwell Books, Secaucus, NJ, 1988

Putnam, Robert D., *Bowling Alone: The Collapse and Revival of American Community*, Simon and Schuster, New York, NY, 2000

RavenWolf, Silver, *American Folk Magick: Charms, Spells and Herbals*, Llewellyn Publications, St. Paul, MN, 1998

Robacker, Earl F., *Pennsylvania Dutch*, University of Pennsylvania Press, Philadelphia, PA, 1944

Roth Teleki, Gloria, *The Baskets of Rural America*, E.P. Dutton Publishers, New York, NY, 1975

Rushing, Felder, *Scarecrows: Making Harvest Figures and Other Yard Folks*, Storey Books, Pownal, VT, 1998

Sabine, Ellen S., *A Treasury of American Folk Patterns*, Van Nostrand Reinhold Company, New York, NY, 1956

Schaut, Jim and Nancy, *Collecting the Old West*, Krause Publications, Iola, WI, 1999

Schneider, Richard C., *Crafts of the Native American Indians: A Craftsman's Manual*, R. Schneider Publications, Stevens Point, WI, 1972

Sexton, Richard, *American Style: Classic Product Design from Airstream to Zippo*, Chronicle Books, San Francisco, CA, 1987

Sita, Lisa, *Indians of the Southwest: Traditions, History, Legends and Life*, Courage Books: an imprint of Running Press, Philadelphia, PA, 1997

Stone, Lynn M., *Back Roads: Pennsylvania Dutch Country*, The Rourke Corporation, Vero Beach, FL, 1993

Tannahill, Reay, *Food in History*, Crown Trade Paperbacks, New York, NY, 1988

Taylor, Colin F., *Native American Arts and Crafts*, Salamander, Smithmark Publishers, New York, NY, 1995

Thompson-Johnson, Frances, *Antique Baskets and Basketry*, Wallace-Homestead Book Company, Lombard, IL, 1985

Today's Hottest Collectibles, Krause Publications, Iola, WI, 2000

Trandem, Bryan (Ed), *Workshop Tips and Techniques*, Black and Decker Home Improvement Library, Cy DeCosse, Inc., Minnetonka, MN, 1991

Tunis, Edwin, *Colonial Living*, The World Publishing Company, Cleveland, OH, 1957

Underhill, Ruth, *Here Come the Navajo! A History of the Largest Indian Tribe in the United States*, Treasure Chest Publications, Tucson, AZ, 1953

Van Gool, *Gulliver's Travels in Lilliput*, Derrydale Books, New York, NY, 1991

Wendorff, Ruth, *How to Make Cornhusk Dolls*, Arco Publishing Company, New York, NY, 1973

Willson, Steven (Ed), *Popular Mechanics Encyclopedia of Tools and Techniques*, Hearst Books, New York, NY, 1994

Young, Tammy, *The Crafter's Guide to Glues*, Chilton Book Company, Radnor, PA, 1995

About the authors

Mary Lou Santovec is a writer currently living in a small town in southern Wisconsin. She has written on a diverse range of topics for magazines, newsletters and newspapers. A former associate editor of *Dollhouse Miniatures* magazine, she is a regular contributor to *Miniature Collector* magazine. She is also coauthor of *1,001 Misspelled Words: What Your Spell Checker Won't Tell You* published by McGraw Hill.

JoAnn Ogreenc is a miniatures artisan currently living in a log cabin in Wisconsin. She and her husband, Jim, have been involved in the miniatures industry since 1989 when they introduced their own line of 1/12 scale architectural details.

Index

GMC Publications

BOOKS

WOODCARVING

The Art of the Woodcarver	*GMC Publications*
Beginning Woodcarving	*GMC Publications*
Carving Architectural Detail in Wood: The Classical Tradition	
	Frederick Wilbur
Carving Birds & Beasts	*GMC Publications*
Carving the Human Figure: Studies in Wood and Stone	
	Dick Onians
Carving Nature: Wildlife Studies in Wood	*Frank Fox-Wilson*
Carving Realistic Birds	*David Tippey*
Decorative Woodcarving	*Jeremy Williams*
Elements of Woodcarving	*Chris Pye*
Essential Woodcarving Techniques	*Dick Onians*
Lettercarving in Wood: A Practical Course	*Chris Pye*
Making & Using Working Drawings for Realistic	
Model Animals	*Basil F. Fordham*
Power Tools for Woodcarving	*David Tippey*
Relief Carving in Wood: A Practical Introduction	*Chris Pye*
Understanding Woodcarving	*GMC Publications*
Understanding Woodcarving in the Round	*GMC Publications*
Useful Techniques for Woodcarvers	*GMC Publications*
Wildfowl Carving – Volume 1	*Jim Pearce*
Wildfowl Carving – Volume 2	*Jim Pearce*
Woodcarving: A Complete Course	*Ron Butterfield*
Woodcarving: A Foundation Course	*Zoë Gertner*
Woodcarving for Beginners	*GMC Publications*
Woodcarving Tools & Equipment Test Reports	*GMC Publications*
Woodcarving Tools, Materials & Equipment	*Chris Pye*

WOODTURNING

Adventures in Woodturning	*David Springett*
Bert Marsh: Woodturner	*Bert Marsh*
Bowl Turning Techniques Masterclass	*Tony Boase*
Colouring Techniques for Woodturners	*Jan Sanders*
Contemporary Turned Wood: New Perspectives	
in a Rich Tradition	*Ray Leier, Jan Peters & Kevin Wallace*
The Craftsman Woodturner	*Peter Child*
Decorating Turned Wood: The Maker's Eye	
	Liz & Michael O'Donnell
Decorative Techniques for Woodturners	*Hilary Bowen*
Fun at the Lathe	*R.C. Bell*
Illustrated Woodturning Techniques	*John Hunnex*
Intermediate Woodturning Projects	*GMC Publications*
Keith Rowley's Woodturning Projects	*Keith Rowley*
Making Screw Threads in Wood	*Fred Holder*
Turned Boxes: 50 Designs	*Chris Stott*

Turning Green Wood	*Michael O'Donnell*
Turning Miniatures in Wood	*John Sainsbury*
Turning Pens and Pencils	*Kip Christensen & Rex Burningham*
Understanding Woodturning	*Ann & Bob Phillips*
Useful Techniques for Woodturners	*GMC Publications*
Useful Woodturning Projects	*GMC Publications*
Woodturning: Bowls, Platters, Hollow Forms, Vases,	
Vessels, Bottles, Flasks, Tankards, Plates	*GMC Publications*
Woodturning: A Foundation Course (New Edition)	*Keith Rowley*
Woodturning: A Fresh Approach	*Robert Chapman*
Woodturning: An Individual Approach	*Dave Regester*
Woodturning: A Source Book of Shapes	*John Hunnex*
Woodturning Jewellery	*Hilary Bowen*
Woodturning Masterclass	*Tony Boase*
Woodturning Techniques	*GMC Publications*
Woodturning Tools & Equipment Test Reports	*GMC Publications*
Woodturning Wizardry	*David Springett*

WOODWORKING

Advanced Scrollsaw Projects	*GMC Publications*
Beginning Picture Marquetry	*Lawrence Threadgold*
Bird Boxes and Feeders for the Garden	*Dave Mackenzie*
Complete Woodfinishing	*Ian Hosker*
David Charlesworth's Furniture-Making Techniques– Volume One	
	David Charlesworth
David Charlesworth's Furniture-Making Techniques – Volume Two	
	David Charlesworth
The Encyclopedia of Joint Making	*Terrie Noll*
Furniture-Making Projects for the Wood Craftsman	
	GMC Publications
Furniture-Making Techniques for the Wood Craftsman	
	GMC Publications
Furniture Projects	*Rod Wales*
Furniture Restoration (Practical Crafts)	*Kevin Jan Bonner*
Furniture Restoration: A Professional at Work	*John Lloyd*
Furniture Restoration and Repair for Beginners	*Kevin Jan Bonner*
Furniture Restoration Workshop	*Kevin Jan Bonner*
Green Woodwork	*Mike Abbott*
The History of Furniture	*Michael Huntley*
Intarsia: 30 Patterns for the Scrollsaw	*John Everett*
Kevin Ley's Furniture Projects	*Kevin Ley*
Making & Modifying Woodworking Tools	*Jim Kingshott*
Making Chairs and Tables	*GMC Publications*
Making Chairs and Tables – Volume 2	*GMC Publications*
Making Classic English Furniture	*Paul Richardson*
Making Heirloom Boxes	*Peter Lloyd*
Making Little Boxes from Wood	*John Bennett*

GARDENING

PHOTOGRAPHY

MAGAZINES

WOODTURNING ◆ WOODCARVING
FURNITURE & CABINETMAKING
THE ROUTER ◆ WOODWORKING
THE DOLLS' HOUSE MAGAZINE
OUTDOOR PHOTOGRAPHY
BLACK & WHITE PHOTOGRAPHY
BUSINESSMATTERS

The above represents a full list of all titles currently published or scheduled to be published. All are available direct from the Publishers or through bookshops, newsagents and specialist retailers. To place an order, or to obtain a complete catalogue, contact:

GMC Publications,
Castle Place, 166 High Street, Lewes,
East Sussex BN7 1XU, United Kingdom
Tel: 01273 488005   Fax: 01273 478606
E-mail: pubs@thegmcgroup.com

Orders by credit card are accepted